PRAISE FOR *THE DESIRE MAP*

"When I sat down with *The Desire Map,* I immediately felt my shoulders relax. Within the first few pages I was nodding my head. I felt heard and validated. She did it. She gets it. And now everyone else can too. I WISH that this goldmine of insight and practical guidance had been by my side over the years. I feel blessed to have Danielle in my life, and I can't wait to see the floodgates of bliss, a-ha's and life-changing shifts burst open as people put their Desire Map into practice. Danielle is a master. She's part psychic, part dream whisperer, and all fire-starter. If you're ready to awaken and live in alignment with who you truly are, then toss your Type-A to-dos and dive heartfirst into *The Desire Map.*"

KRIS CARR
author of *Crazy Sexy Kitchen* and *Crazy Sexy Diet*

"The Desire Map has such life, truth, and passion; what could be better than realigning yourself daily with your heart's desire?

GENEEN ROTH
author *Women, Food, and God* and *Lost and Found*

"With an organic elegance, *The Desire Map* couples our primal desire-energy with the inborn intelligence of our feelings. The result? Optimizing our time on Earth. LaPorte's *joie de vivre* is contagious. Prepare to catch it!"

MICHAEL BERNARD BECKWITH
author of *Life Visioning*

"The first time I did a Desire Map, I called Danielle to say, 'This works!' Declaring my core desired feelings uplifted my relationships and the way I work in the world. And nobody puts out poetic motivation like Danielle does. *The Desire Map* is a hotline to your truth."

GABRIELLE BERNSTEIN
author of *May Cause Miracles* and *Spirit Junkie*

"Danielle LaPorte is scary smart, yet so kind and practical that she kindles the fire in you without causing you to feel consumed by the flames. She has the knowledge you need to succeed. Lean in and listen close. What she has to say is what our spirits need to hear."

MARTHA BECK
author of *Finding Your Own North Star* and *The Joy Diet*

"Danielle is a yoga-powered champion of YOU-ness. That is . . . you, rocking your mission and brimming with desire. And *The Desire Map* lays out the roadmap for how to rewire your desire, not stress. She has accomplished something extraordinary."

SARA GOTTFRIED, MD
author of *The Hormone Cure*

"Inspiration, innovation, and self-worth are just some of elements that Danielle LaPorte will fill you up with. *The Desire Map* discusses how to make your dreams and goals come true in a realistic way . . . guaranteed to wow you."

BELIEFNET.COM

"As always, Danielle LaPorte has broken the mold for self-actualization with *The Desire Map.* This experience will invite, challenge, and even seduce you to get to know the core of who you are. *The Desire Map* doesn't give you some sort of outside-in prescription to 'live your dreams' and 'tackle lofty goals' like other programs. Instead, you'll be guided through a process that's guaranteed to help you craft your life and make decisions based on what will truly make you happy. Forget time-management systems, goal-setting programs, and visioning exercises. *The Desire Map* is all you need to design a life that will truly work for you."

KATE NORTHRUP
author of *Money: A Love Story*

"*The Desire Map* has me reeling. Your truth is so laid bare, raw, revealed. I'm drop-jawed in awe."

MEGGAN WATTERSON
author of *Reveal: A Sacred Manual for Getting Spiritually Naked*

"I'm only on page 11 of *The Desire Map* and my mind has been blown WIDE OPEN."

GALA DARLING
GalaDarling.com

"I've lived in overdrive. For years. I was a tenacious goal-getter and I drove myself hard to reach those goals—no matter what they were. Until I hit a wall and thought, 'There's gotta be another way.' *The Desire Map* is that 'other way.' This is what people are looking for—a new way to plan their lives, an inside-out approach."

ERIC HANDLER
PositivelyPositive.com

"Most of us are so busy planning that we forget what we're planning for. Danielle LaPorte has ignited a reverence for our desires in a way that brings meaning back to our daily actions. *The Desire Map* is a life-changer."

NISHA MOODLEY
FierceFabulousFree.com

"My only mistake was starting to read *The Desire Map* at night. I couldn't put it down, madly scouring my heart for longing, writing down my desires with clarity I haven't felt for years. It's straightforward and yet deeply poetic. It's big and beautiful and generous and profound. I don't say this lightly—it changes everything."

SAMANTHA REYNOLDS
founder and president, Echo Memoirs

"*The Desire Map.* It's a motherload of motivation, inspiration, and transformative triggers to help you start living the life of your dreams as an entrepreneur, a lover, a hero. Under its gorgeous cover, it's packed with videos, fantastic music tracks, contemplations, workbooks, and Danielle's famed street-smart wisdom."

NAVJIT KANDOLA
TenderLogic.com

The
Desire
Map

ALSO BY DANIELLE LAPORTE

The Fire Starter Sessions: A Soulful + Practical Guide to Creating Success on Your Own Terms

DESIRE MAP RESOURCES

There is a small multimedia universe of Desire Map materials to help you make this a practice in your life. In addition to this book, numerous audio programs are available as well as a printed day planner, journal, and smaller versions of the workbook. There is also a Facebook group, digital posters, music playlists, group meeting resources, and a Desire Map online subscription service. Head to DanielleLaPorte.com to explore.

Want to start your own Desire Map group? You can partake in the world's biggest book club ever. Go to DanielleLaPorte.com/bookclub.

FOLLOW DANIELLE LAPORTE

DanielleLaPorte.com

FACEBOOK
daniellelaporte.com/facebook

TWITTER
#desiremap, @daniellelaporte

PINTEREST
pinterest.com/daniellelaporte

INSTAGRAM
instagram.com/daniellelaporte

The Desire Map

A GUIDE TO CREATING GOALS WITH SOUL

DANIELLE LAPORTE

sounds true
BOULDER, COLORADO

Sounds True, Inc.

Boulder, CO 80306

Published 2014

Cover design by Danielle LaPorte, Alex Miles Younger, Angie Wheeler,
Viewers Like You

Book design by Alex Miles Younger

Printed in Canada

Library of Congress Cataloging-in-Publication Data
LaPorte, Danielle, 1969–
  The desire map : a guide to creating goals with soul / Danielle LaPorte.
    pages cm
  ISBN 978-1-62203-251-8
  1. Goal (Psychology) 2. Self-realization. 3. Satisfaction. I. Title.
  BF503.L365 2014
  153.8'5—dc23
                                        2013035366

Ebook ISBN: 978-1-62203-346-1

Enhanced ebook ISBN: 978-1-62203-377-5

10 9 8 7 6 5 4 3 2 1

for
you

certain wondering lost found here
hungry full of love
waking up down
been around
more than you were yesterday
already new
true
scars of knowing
always growing
more
light
right
now

for
you

As is your desire, so is your will.
As is your will, so is your deed.
As is your deed,
so is your destiny.

—The Upanishads

BOOK ONE: THE THEORY

Book One:
The Theory

THE VISTA: PROGRAM OVERVIEW

If you begin to understand what you are without trying to change it,
then what you are undergoes a transformation.

—Jiddu Krishnamurti

IT ALL BEGAN ON NEW YEAR'S EVE, BY THE FIRE

About eight years ago, I decided to have a chill New Year's Eve at home. The scene: The baby was sleeping (Yay!). Favorite white trashy snackies (Ruffles chips and ranch dip, please). Groove Armada on the speakers. Fireplace blazing. The New Year was wide open and my heart was full of ambition. It was time for some visioning. Goals! Plans! Lots of plans.

I pulled out some poster board and divided it into some life sections, like Home, Love, Money, Work. My former husband and I started writing down goals in each area. We'd write a goal, have a smooch, eat some chips, talk about the next goal. *New kitchen table. Pay off credit card. Water Babies swim class. Lose ten pounds. Invest in a great piece of art. Start biking to work. Hawaii for family wedding. Get the garden happening. Down payment. Publishing deal. New Frye boots. Find a church. Find a yoga class.*

Him: Maybe we should go to Australia while it's easy to travel with the baby.

Me: *(I have no interest in going to Australia with a baby. So I deflect.)* Do you think Dick Clark is going to show up for the ball drop tonight, or is Ryan Seacrest doing the whole thing?

(pause)

I'm so done with this sofa. It's too big for this room. Let's get a new sofa!

Him: But I love this sofa.

Me: I want the new MacBook Pro! With mega ram jam.

Him: Yah, you deserve some new gear, babe.

Me: I do, don't I?

It wasn't quite a vision board, but it wasn't just a to-do list. And yet something was still missing. It felt full, but empty. Eager but not . . . *energizing*. I pulled out a different colored pen and started scrawling positive feeling words in each section.

Freedom!
Abundance.
Sexy.
Earth. Nature. Eco-love.
Connected.
Creative.
Temple.
True love.

Me: How do you wanna feel at work?

Him: Courageous. Confident. Adventurous.

And things shifted. The exercise turned inside out. So we started it over.

Instead of talking about external goals, we talked about how we wanted to feel in the various parts of our lives.

The process was more engaging. And our list of wants started to morph.

Have a dinner party once a month.
Get a KitchenAid mixer—make pasta.
Design a line of thank-you cards.
Download Tantra CDs.
Two-week canoe trip.
Self-publish.

Visually, it started to look more beautiful. Psychologically, it felt like an invitation instead of another list of things to do.

Jump-cut to a few more New Years passed. Fireplace lit. Ryan Seacrest standing in for Dick Clark. The "feelings 'n' goals thing," as it came to be known, had evolved into an unofficial process that was making a difference in how we looked at the future.

We wrote out a bunch of positive feelings, and then we asked ourselves, **"So what can we do to feel that way?"**

In that simple question lay a new way of living life, which subtly and slowly led to profound changes in the way I went about getting things done. I officially gave up goal-setting systems, which eventually led to quitting to-do lists, which led to giving up the time-management systems that were totally stressing me out.

Revelation dawning. Focusing on desired feelings = liberated energy. I was onto something.

At the end of the year when I'd review my "vision poster thing," as it was also known at the time, I didn't feel so disappointed in myself when I hadn't checked off *Paris* or *Lose ten pounds* as accomplishments on the list. I looked at things differently. I could see that my two trips to New York that year and the new yoga classes were fulfilling my longed-for states of being. I was making progress. I was feeling the way I wanted to feel more often than not.

This way of life planning was more fluid and compassionate, and ironically, it was also more motivating. Just as I could see how unmet goals were synchronistically replaced by other happenings—often better than the ones I had imagined—I could also see where I was out of alignment with my truest desires. I could see that I wasn't feeling, say, very free, or as creative or connected as I wanted to feel in certain areas of my life.

I took the exercise into the rest of the year. I revisited my plans in May for my birthday, and in September, because I love the "let's get cozy and get down to business" energy of autumn. As *The Happiness Project* author, Gretchen Rubin, puts it, "September is the new January."

I took the exercise deeper. I began to actually meditate on the words themselves. I looked up definitions and origins of various words and started to winnow them down. Four feelings to focus on felt manageable and inspiring. And then, ladies and gentlemen, **I created . . . The Sticky Note . . . that would change everything.** Four feelings. Stuck in my Day-Timer. Referred to every day. Guiding my choices.

I started speaking about the Desired Feelings Thing, as it became known, onstage at my speaking gigs. "So when you get clear on how you actually want to feel, your life-planning process might get turned upside down," I explained. And chicks would come up to me afterward: "So how do I do that 'Desired Feelings thing'?" "Oh my God, you're so right about your feelings and goals. I've always felt that way. Is there a worksheet I can get?" We were onto something.

I gave the theory a name: The Strategy of Desire. I wrote about it in session 3 of my book, *The Fire Starter Sessions,* and it proved to be the most meaningfully discussed chapter of the book. Feedback started rolling in. People were posting pictures of their core desired feelings in their journals and on fridges. Facebook discussions. Tweeted "feelings lists."

In the meantime, I started working even more deeply with the process. As a meditation; as a system; as an exploration of my own relationship with desire itself; as a prayer . . . as a multimedia sermon on making more empowered choices.

And then I decided to make this really real in the world and released *The Desire Map* program to my readers. And then it was really undeniable: people are craving a new way to make things happens in their lives. Less driving and more inspiration. Deeper meaning but without compromising prosperity. More love and way less judgment.

And the stories . . . the stories slayed me. Quitting jobs or doing work very very differently. Getting closer to significant others and getting closer to major personal truth. Whether someone writes me about what they were stopping or beginning, or the paradigm that they'd cracked open for themselves, one thing is gloriously clear: when you lean into your desires, you liberate your power—and your joy.

Welcome to *The Desire Map.*

THE GUIDING PREMISE

We have the procedures of achievement upside down. Typically we come up with our to-do lists, our bucket lists, and our strategic plans—all the stuff we want to have, get, accomplish, and experience outside of ourselves. All of those aspirations are being driven by an innate desire to feel a certain way.

So what if, first, we got clear on how we actually wanted to feel within ourselves, and then we designed our to-do lists, set our goals, and wrote out our bucket lists?

How do you want to feel when you look at your schedule for the week? When you get dressed in the morning? When you walk through the door of your studio or your office? When you pick up the phone? When you cash the check, accept the award, finish your masterpiece, make the sale, or fall in love?

How do you want to feel?

Knowing how you actually want to feel is the most potent form of clarity that you can have. Generating those feelings is the most powerfully creative thing you can do with your life.

—from "Session 3: The Strategy of Desire," *The Fire Starter Sessions*

IDEAS. INTROSPECTION. CLARITY. ACTION.

This is two books in one. One part is the theory: the root of desire, the power of feelings, the perils and promise of intentions and goals. And one part is the methodology: an actual workbook that helps you clarify **how you want to feel** in your life, and **what you want to do, have, and experience** in alignment with those feelings.

You could call it holistic life planning. The inner meets the outer. The spirit drives the material.

The purpose of *The Desire Map* is:

› Ultimately, to help you **remember your light**, your true nature, your source—the life source that connects us all

› To show you your heart's longing—**your core desired feelings**

› To guide you in using **your preferred feelings as a guidance system for making choices** and for being more present and alive

› To help you use your desired feelings as a way to **access comfort and clarity during painful times**

› To show you how to use your desired feelings as **creative fuel** to make great things happen in your life that will radiate out into the world

› To help you **accentuate the positive** aspects of your life, while still honoring, and not invalidating, the negative parts that you want to change

› To help you realize that you are much bigger than your feelings, and also, perhaps paradoxically, to help you regard your **feelings as road signs to your Soul**

The Desire Map is designed to help you make more empowered choices.

Which is to say both to **make *more* choices in your life** and to **make choices that are more *empowered*.**

You have a say in your life. There is so much that we can intentionally select in creating our reality. What comes into our cupboards and closets, what goes into our bodies, the people with whom we spend our free time, the gifts we give, how we worship, the thoughts we focus on. Clutter is a choice. Anger is a choice. Resentment is a choice. So are spaciousness, flexibility, laughter, compassion, tenderness, and resilience.

Empowered choices are "whole choices" that take your mind, body, and Soul into consideration. These decisions include our personal ecology— how much time we have, how it feels to give that time, where our wounds and sensitivities reside, where our strengths meet the needs of the world. When we are choosing from a whole place, we're aware of how our decisions bring us closer to or further from ourselves, each other, and society.

If you put *The Desire Map* to practical use:

> when you're coming up with your yearly goals, planning your week, building your career, making holiday plans . . . *you'll have your core desired feelings in mind;*

> when you're choosing whom to invite in, how to react, what to give, where to go, how to move, how and what you'll worship . . . *you'll have your core desired feelings in mind;*

> when you want things to be different, when you're in pain, when you've got a great idea to act on, when you want to make stuff . . . *you'll have your core desired feelings in mind;*

> when you're composing the email, asking for what you want, choosing presents, shopping for shoes . . . *you'll have your core desired feelings in mind;*

> when you go to sleep at night, and you wake up in the morning . . . *you'll have your core desired feelings in mind.*

And what you have in mind is how you create your reality.

This has got to be practical. I can give you poetic theories and motivational pump-up, but if you can't use this on a day-to-day basis to feel better, then we've missed the mark. I, for one, am very results-oriented—the greatest result being that I feel connected to my energy source more often than I feel separate from it. And that requires daily awareness and openness—in the kitchen, in emails, in conversation, at the grocery store.

PLANNING YOUR DAY TURNS INTO LIVING YOUR LIFE

Most life-planning tools focus on external attainment and results—on accomplishments. Which is incredibly valuable. Aiming for results is what moves your life forward. Except that most goal-setting systems fail to harness the most powerful driver behind any pursuit: your most desired feelings.

> You're not chasing the goal itself—you're chasing the feelings that you hope attaining those goals will give you.

You may not even be conscious of this. Many of us are on achievement autopilot. I walked into the lobby of a major corporation and the staff had their five-year goals posted everywhere. *Married with 2 kids by 34. I am living on the ocean and loving the view! Get my MBA! I finish top of my age group in the marathon. I will be traveling the world and earning a living teaching. In 5 years I will launch my own clothing line.*

Cool. All those things are awesome to have. Most of us live in a veritable paradise of privileges—even if our resources are few, the vast majority of us have access to amazing opportunities and social nourishment. Go for whatever you want—just know why you're going after it. Because if you're going to business school so that your dad will pat you on the back at graduation and you'll feel respectable and strong, or you're planning to buy a house with hardwood floors because it's going to make you feel a sense of peace, you may be looking for love in all the wrong, well, goals.

When you get clear on how you want to feel, you may find yourself going after different things, and you may find yourself going after them in a different way.

When you get clear on how you want to feel, your external goals can shift into a more comfortable place in your psyche and you will likely feel much more integrated.

When you get clear on how you want to feel, the pursuit itself becomes more satisfying. The quality of the journey and the destination begin to merge in your heart.

This program is not:

› About planning out the next decade or your whole entire life. Five-year plans are critical for businesses and companies. Here, we're starting with your heart—which will dictate what you want to make in the world, and therefore also guide your five-year plans if and when you need to make them. But we're looking at a year at a time. Personally, I like to create a new Desire Map for myself twice a year.

› A tool for project management. You need a project-management tool for that.

› A new time-management or calendar system. Because the world does not need another time-management or calendar system. And because there are already some excellent systems out there.

***The Desire Map* is an ideology that fits into any beloved calendar or goal system that you are already using. It's the horse that pulls the cart.**

Make this yours, please.

All of it is open to your interpretation—there is no right or wrong way to do this. Start where you want. Say what you need to say.

You could:
Do it all at once and run your own Soul marathon.
Create a staycation retreat—three afternoons of introspection and visioning.
Take as many weeks as you need.
Do it once a year.

Come back to it every Sunday.

Form a group.

Take the day off work and do it on your birthday.

Start every new year with a Desire Map.

When you get clear on how you want to feel, the pursuit itself will become more satisfying.

Light to
Steer By

INTRODUCING: DESIRE. THE MOST CREATIVE FORCE IN THE UNIVERSE.

Look into the nature of desire, and there is boundless light.

—Padmasambhava, Tibetan yogi

THE

ESSENCE

OF YOUR

DESIRE IS

A FEELING

Life-affirming desires. Latent desires. Secret desires. Abandoned, neglected, avoided desires. Rescued. Feral. Inextinguishable. Set-your-Soul-on-fire desires.

Never underestimate the power of wanting.

You want it and you want it bad. Aspiring. Hoping. Plotting. Recurring. Reaching. Bubbling beneath your surface. You crave it and it craves you.

So you make a plan to get it. The goal. The bucket list. Quarterly objectives. Strategy. Accountability. Mission: Possible.

And then you pray, assume, yearn, and hope that you'll feel good when you get what you want.

Desire is the engine of creation.

It is the apex of our expanding consciousness. It infuses us with the courage to do the most noble acts, to sacrifice, and pursue, and wrest ourselves away from darkness to move into the light. It can drive us to madness, despair, and disabling doubt. Desire steers our pleasure pursuits of food, sex, joy, self-expression, and connection. Through our wanting, we come to know more of ourselves, each other, and life.

Desire is at the root of our divine impulse to evolve.

Desire leads the way home.

THE POUNDING HEART OF LIBERATION

So I once sent an email to a lama. A Tibetan Buddhist lama. Let's call him Lama M. I was high off of a weekend workshop with him and other Buddhists and wannabe Buddhists. For the record, I'm neither. And FYI, if you're neither a Buddhist nor an aspiring Buddhist, and you show up at a Buddhist intensive, you *will* feel like a retreat crasher. Go anyway, should the opportunity present itself. When they're chanting in Sanskrit, just murmur right along. Back to the cushion. All those mantras had expanded my mind, I was seeing sacred shapes when I closed my eyes, my heart was aching with relief, and I was ready to get down to some further philosophical business.

On 2010-07-04, at 10:00 a.m., Danielle LaPorte wrote:

Dearest Lama M,

I'm very curious about "desiring" enlightenment. Christians (my family of origin) have that passion that drives them. It's that wretched longing for communion—which I think is often more about getting approval than achieving genuine connection. There's something under that drive—something mixed up in wanting desperately to be free of suffering, and at the same time to be One. There's something not quite right about this striving approach. At least, not for me.

I want (badly) to be free of certain things like, say, the warrior loneliness and perpetual self-judgment that I experience, for starters . . . But I wonder if that intense wanting to be "better" is the wrong way to go about things.

Perhaps it's about letting my essence, my Buddha nature, just be revealed.

I have a fire, this passion, this hunger, this drrrrive—all useful forces in how I make things happen (and I make a lot of things happen, quickly). Those seem to be characteristics of devotion. So then it becomes a matter of what I'm devoted to. Or, is it about my relationship to devotion—to what I desire?

The fine point, my actual question: ***What is the "right" energy of desiring enlightenment?***

Is this a good place to begin?

I am sending much love from here to there.

Respectfully and deeply grateful,
Danielle

Re: the business of dharma: Um . . . do you take PayPal? Please let me know how I can reciprocate in my human way for your teaching. Dana, right? Good old-fashioned donation?

Lama M got back to me right away. And FYI, he refused to take a donation. It went something like this:

Hello Danielle,

All good questions! [Note: this immediate affirmation from Lama M instantly made me feel like a "good student." He likes me! My ego was stoked. We were off to a good start.]

"Your question is at the heart of liberation; how to want, have an aim or goal, but not be in a state of desire or clinging. The simple advice is: you can't! There is desire."

Yet, the art is to have a "deep" desire to want liberation or freedom from afflictive states, as this is the "stream" or "current" that moves the being in the right direction . . .

The art of it is to keep asking yourself quietly: Am I being pushy? Is my desire for freedom clean or is it tainted with all kinds of emotional overtones? In my desire to be free, am I harming myself or others around me? Am I making a weird trip out of life, or living life naturally and cleanly? In other words, how neurotic (frozen, harming, non-functional) are my actions, speech (all forms of communication), and thoughts around liberation or awakening?

I reread his letter a dozen times. So let's review: We are naturally going to desire things, enlightenment, even. Having deep desire for freedom is an especially good thing—it moves us in the right direction, closer to our true nature. But if we're a neurotic mess or a pushy mofo with regard to our spiritual longings, it all kind of backfires. You with me so far?

Lama M then reconfirmed my previously assigned duty: to visualize and recite 100,000 times the Prajna Paramita Heart Sutra and call him in the morning. He also attached a prayer from St. John of the Cross that he felt "spoke beautifully to the nature of desire." A refrain:

> To reach satisfaction in all
> desire its possession in nothing,
> To come to the knowledge of all
> desire the knowledge of nothing.
> To come to possess all
> desire the possession of nothing.
> To arrive at being all
> desire to be nothing.
>
> —St. John of the Cross

Translation: Want it with all your heart. But don't get attached to getting it.

Tricky. Very tricky.

So, clearly, it was time for me to get into a healthier relationship with desire itself—to get into a place of continuing to have strong desires but also have more surrender around them. I decided that if I wanted a shift in *how* I desired, then maybe I should start looking at *what* I desired. And I might as well keep digging into **the *why* behind my desires.**

What I desire:

I desire to write, be wildly in love, support my son to be who he is, keep my hair thick and shiny, get more tattoos, recite mantras, speak onstage, sleep in linen sheets, drive alone in the wide open spaces of New Mexico for hours, be flexible and productive, be alone at parties, be alone at home, be alone, be liked-loved-respected, keep a temple-tidy house, drive a reliable car, make millions of dollars and give lots away, meditate, get caught in thunderstorms, dance long and hard, wear cashmere, make things that make people want to make things of their own, sleep in, recycle, be One, seek approval, go to weddings (and funerals), order in, worship Rothko paintings, call my grandmother, free spiders, go back to India, stay up too late, get just the right font spacing, listen to Tibetan singing bowls on repeat for hours, watch three documentaries in a row, give all I have to give at any given moment to pretty much anybody, wear perfume every day of the week, shave my head, burn everything I've ever written, give insight, give money, give time, find my True Nature, and touch the face of God . . .

Why do I desire what I desire?

The answer is fast, clear, and simple: **to feel good, of course.**

LOOK DESIRE IN THE EYE

Desire is a teacher: When we immerse ourselves in it
without guilt, shame or clinging, it can show us something special
about our own minds that allows us to embrace life fully.

—Mark Epstein, *Open to Desire*

Something phenomenal happens when you start to examine your desires. You get closer to your current reality—all that you can appreciate, and everything you want to change. And you also get closer to your potential. You see the dark side of your clinging, all those things that you're hammering away at to get—the neediness and the impulse to make demands on the world. And, mercifully, you can see the purity of your longing—all that's natural and good and divine about what you want out of life.

Desire is the foundation of our will to live. When you cease to desire, you cease to evolve. Your pursuit of the things you want can shift from feverish and anxiety-driven to trusting and fluid. But even with a more liberated consciousness, desire remains the mesh underlying our material existence and our spiritual growth.

When I close my eyes for a minute and consider what I want the most, when I lean into my longings, I get the image of being in a sacred kind of egg where absolutely anything is possible, and at the same time, everything is so stunningly fragile. I become aware of a longing that exists everywhere—in my body, mind, and spirit—in my pounding heart, within my personality, and in the expanse of my Soul.

Desire hurts so good. It is an ache that we will never escape, nor would we want to if we want to be fully alive. When we numb out our natural longings, it affects all of our senses. Even if it seems like it's taking too long for what we want to arrive, it's better to stay with the ache than abandon the desire. Feel your way through.

Your desire is revealing. Have a straightforward conversation with it. It's likely to tell you that you want X because it will make you feel *complete*. Or that you want Y because it will make you feel *powerful*. Or that you want Z because it will make you feel *free*.

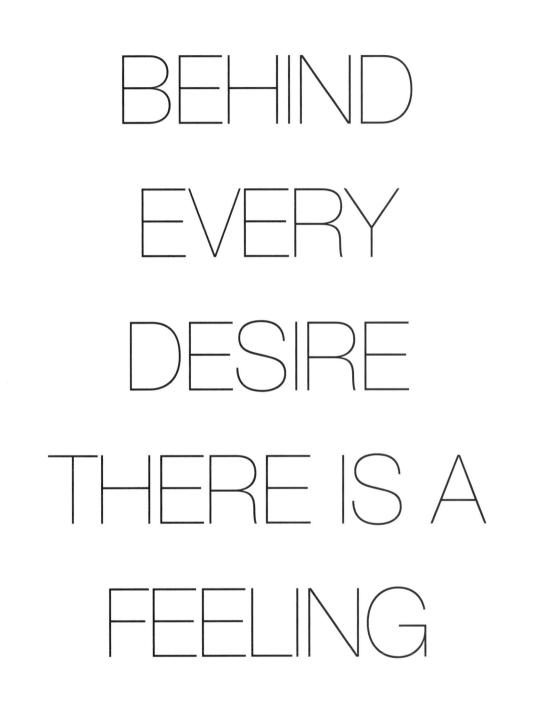

AND YOUR
FEELINGS
WILL LEAD
YOU TO
YOUR SOUL

We're here for some desire analysis. Sigmund Freud called it psychotherapy. I just want you to know how you want to feel.

Clinging or trusting? Austere or hedonistic? Ego-based or Soul-driven? You can spend years psychoanalyzing your relationship to desire and how you go after what you want. I'm a fan of psychotherapy. Just ask my shrinks—all seven that I've had over the years. And I think everyone could do with a few years of therapeutic, shamanic, somatic release; astral traveling; dream analysis; meditative, energetic, craniosacral, past-life regression; mind-state dabbling; and deep Soul-diving exploration. However . . .

I'm also a pragmatist—and often in a rush. And I want to be happy—as much as possible, as soon as possible. And I know I'm not the only one.

So let's talk in terms of Soul practicality. The day-to-day sacred. Getting the right stuff done, without delay.

Let's get straight to what we all want: **To feel good, of course.**

HOW DO YOU WANT TO FEEL?
I ASKED. YOU ANSWERED:

Inspired. Secure. Turned on (intellectually, I mean). :) / En route / ALIVE / I want to feel like a Rumi poem. / Tantric priestess of life! / Like this / Fulfilled / Energized / Embodied and nourished / Like I matter / Alive and overflowing with abundance of all that I desire! / Delighted with life / Energized / Full of life and full of ENERGY!!! / fully incarnate, magical / At peace / Your sister in value and passion / Turned on / Energized, delighted / Like an orgasm / Calm and relaxed / Bold. Connected. Empowered with superpowers to accomplish it all. / Safe. Loved. Happy. All the things I've finally found. :) / Secure / Limitless! / Unburdened / Fearless / Effective, shiny, unencumbered, and ready / Free, Empowered, Expansive, Abundant, Valuable, Vibrant, Sexy, Strong, Luxurious, Unstoppable! / Interested / Fully / Fully expressed / Authentically brilliant! / Calm, inspired, in the flow, abundant / Vibrant! Turned on! Powerful! / energetic. inspired. fearless. / Easy like Sunday morn' / Whole / Elated / In my flow. Peaceful. Beaming love. Abundant. / Free / I want to feel generous. / Authentic. Genuine. Peaceful. / Like a bright blessing . . . / Awake / Lit UP / Juicy / AWESOME!!!!! / Ecstatic (or maybe there should be an exclamation point there . . . ecstatic!) / Full of expanding fiery bliss / Free! / Vibrant / Enraptured. Creative. Solid. Beautiful. Grateful. / Competent / Alive with fire and purpose / energetic / Happy / Innovative. Caring. Generous. / Vibrant . . . great word! / Content. To be able to know—and say—"Yes. This is what I want." / At ease with anything I'm feeling / Balanced between grounded and happily excited and full of energy. Staying grounded is my challenge! / Radiant. Light. Purposeful. / clear, strong, bright. Always. / Flowing! Masterful. Like I just remembered something that is SO important and now SO CLEAR & it's making me LAUGH. ♥ / Empowered / Connected to the divine spirit within me and within us all ♥ / Happy / Joyful / Alive / Total body relaxation and support / Fulfilled. Strong. Clear. / Centered. / Inspired. Guided. Purposeful. / Accomplished! / Free / Alive. Invigorated. Excited. / Pumped / Unabashedly vulnerable at all times / Like I can do anything / Fearless / Inspired / Balanced, at peace, and flowing love :) / Blessed / Relieved. I think it's my favorite feeling. / At peace / :) like this :) HAPPY / Fired up and passionate / Like a rock star! / On top of the world euphoric being! / Radiant / Unencumbered with a feathery concern / Healthy / Unstuck / Like the driver, not the passenger / Free / Full of possibility of aliveness, vitality, love, and joy / Free from being overwhelmed! Happy, joyous & free, motivated, successful & financially content ♥ / Capable. Powerful. Helpful. Loved. / Peaceful and full of bliss in a calm, knowing way / Alive / Challenged, yet in flow . . . fiery, yet peaceful . . . with a cherry of blissful happiness on top :) / Free and Magical / Expansive / Fulfilled / Better / Perfectly centered and peaceful. Saw this phrase in *The Untethered Soul.* Might even get it tatted! / Secure, at peace, energized, fulfilled, and creative (I get to want as many good feelings as I want, right?) / Powerful and one with the universe and its magic / Energized / I want to feel amazing, purposeful, and fulfilled / Awesome / Secure / Peaceful, loved, and a little bit sexy / At peace / That I have as much time as I will ever need up until the day I die / Present in every single moment! / Slightly centered, calm, and clear / I want to feel the bliss of giving money away! / Excited/motivated! / Exuberant / Appreciated, happy, alive / Fully content / Lighter / Open to whatever comes next! / Oh, I did this worksheet! My list is written on my bathroom mirror: Centered, Connected, Appreciated, Anticipative, Affluent. / At ease / Strong . . . in every way / Aligned with my higher self / Free, capable, and easy / Calm and on top of it all / Present, clear-hearted, and divine . . . / Fearless / REAL Beautiful!! ♥ / peaceful, content, loved / Authentic. Empowered. Creative. Nourished. / Enthusiastic, inspired, excited, full of possibility, calm, serene, joyful, useful, helpful, appreciated, and affluent (your word, Danielle—your definition of which resonated deeply with me) / I want to feel "led," led by God, however you like to call him, higher power, the universe. He has all sorts of interesting names these days. There is nothing, no feeling anywhere, anytime that compares to that feeling. / Intensely. Everything. / Happy, loved, and content / In no particular order—energetic, appreciated, passionate, playful, slim, fulfilled, adored, blissfully happy, and debt-free!! / Alive—really deeply, passionately alive / Blissful / Safe enough to risk everything. / Confident (opposite of fearful) / Secure / Everything every minute with endless joy and awe / Peaceful, grounded, and in my power / Healthy and content . . . Rested / Content / Loved / Easy / Like the painter . . . and the painting / Purposeful; filled with purpose & accomplished. Happy, sensual / Like I'm playing / How I feel at this moment . . . happy and flowing with life! / I want to feel vibrant present joyful and alive! / Light, Free, Beautiful, Bright, Joy-filled, Creative, Happy, Accepted, Energetic, Healthy, Loved, Safe, Secure, Independent, Youthful ♥ / Engaged / I want to feel energized! / Relaxed / Appreciated, safe, loved, energized, content! / Valued, validated, and enough from the inside—not based on if I am liked or not . . . / Healthy, affluent, centered, JUBILANT!!!!!! / Inspired! / Worry-free, energized, powerful, and peaceful / Turned on, free, inspiring, powerful, affluent, clear, love

THE MAGNETICS OF FEELINGS

Whenever you start guiding yourself by caring about how you feel,
you start guiding yourself back into your Stream of Source Energy,
and that's where your clarity is; that's where your joy is; that's where your flexibility is;
that's where your balance is; that's where your good ideas come from.
That's where all the good stuff is accessed from.

—Abraham-Hicks

EVERYTHING WE DO IS DRIVEN BY THE DESIRE TO FEEL A CERTAIN WAY

What you buy, what you eat, what you say, who you choose to hang with, the things you make, the people you give your love to, what you wear, what you listen to, what you bring into your home, what you end, begin, and dream of . . . all go back to the desire to feel good.

This applies to all ranges of circumstance. Surviving can be our definition of feeling good, thriving can be our definition of feeling good. Some of us are feeling just good enough to manage our mental health. And some of us are feeling attuned to the pulse of life itself, and that becomes our own version of feeling good.

Sometimes even feeling bad feels good. Negative emotions can feel so familiar to us (especially if they mimic our past) as to actually be comforting. Awareness is realizing that our life could always be better. Growth is doing what it takes to make it better. When we choose the positive over the negative, liberation over repression, truth over illusion, we become real creators.

When we want to feel courageous more than we want to check accomplishments off our list . . . When we want to feel free more than we want to please other people . . . When we want to feel good more than we want to look good . . . then we've got our priorities in order. Divine priorities—the kind that will steer you to the life you long for most deeply.

FEELINGS ARE POWER

Cognitively, we don't locate emotions in our heads; we tend to locate them in our hearts—our fourth chakra. Love, joy, enthusiasm, confidence, tenderness, connection, and even the so-called negative emotions, like sadness, grief, and anger, seem to pour forth from our heart center.

My heart exploded, my heart leapt, my heart sank. He puffed up his chest with pride. She did it wholeheartedly. I knew in my heart.

A feeling is much stronger than a thought.

The heart generates the largest electromagnetic field in the body . . .
The electrical field is about 60 times greater in amplitude than the
brain waves. The magnetic component of the heart's field, which is
around 100 times stronger than that produced by the brain . . .
can be measured several feet away from the body.

—Rollin McCraty, PhD

WE NEED TO MAKE OUR FEELINGS THE HEART OF THE MATTER

Don't take it personally. Keep your feelings in check. Don't let your heart rule your head. Don't wear your heart on your sleeve. Don't get emotionally involved. Don't be so sensitive. Don't let your feelings get the better of you. It doesn't matter how you feel about it—it's the way it is.

In the midst of a messy business divorce, I had an investor tell me "not [to] let my feelings get in the way." "Well, you know, Dick, if I'd let my feelings 'get in the way' a few months ago, I would have spoken up and I wouldn't be in this mess." Word.

But instead, I overrode my feelings. I settled for feeling way less than awesome on a regular basis. At that time in my career, I was seriously out of touch with how I truly *wanted* to feel. I didn't yet have the compass of my core desired feelings, and I drifted in a soup of predominantly negative emotions around my business.

Feelings aren't facts. This is another adage that has us disregard our feelings. And, I happen to agree with it—50 percent agree with it. (Keep reading. We'll talk about the difference between your true self and your emotions in a few pages.)

So-called fact: *He was rude.* So-called fact: *She's beautiful.* Neither are irrefutable "facts" of what happened or of what's true. What's rude in one culture is princely in another; or maybe rude dude thought he was being polite and you just misunderstood. And beauty, as we all know, is widely subjective.

However, your *experience* is true for you!

So-called fact: *I'm angry because he was rude.* So-called fact: *I'm turned on because she's so beautiful.* It's true that you feel whatever way you feel. Who can argue with the fact that you are indeed ticked off or turned on? In this way, your feelings are factual to you. You really feel them. It doesn't matter if you're "right," it doesn't even matter if you're being overly sensitive or narcissistic.

Feelings are neither the facts of what *actually* happened nor of a shared reality. They are indicators of your personal reality. The material facts may be disputable, but the fact that you feel a certain way is not. And that fact is very, very important.

Feelings are how you perceive life. Perception informs how you live.

It's a crime against the human spirit that we so often disassociate positive emotions from the pursuit of success.

We tell ourselves that *it'll be worth it when we get there,* and we grind and crank and endure our way to the goal posts. We man up, suck it up, and shut up—all in the name of making a better life for ourselves. We fake it so we can *be somebody.*

Our productivity- and results-obsessed society pathologizes feelings.

Business and academic cultures are especially adept at discrediting the intelligence of feelings. After all, following your heart is often illogical and seemingly counterproductive. Not too many shareholders are asking, *What's the most joyful way to conduct business?* Scarce are the diet programs and exercise regimens that value happiness or freedom over weight-loss metrics. I'd flip for an investment advisor who asked me, *What makes you feel most connected and excited in terms of where you can put your money?*

Discipline can feel wildly liberating. Shrewd, tactical thinking can feel incredibly creative and energizing. I'm not saying that positive feelings can't exist in pursuit of material goals or within conventional environments. I'm saying that, far too often, epidemically often, we go for the external win at the cost of our internal wellness. And that's because **we don't value inner attunement as much as we value outer attainment.**

WE ALL KNOW THAT PERSON

I spoke at a university event and asked the student organizer what she was going to school for. "Oh, finance," she answered. "So, working with numbers really lights you up, then?" I said. She didn't understand the question. "What do you mean?" she replied. "I mean, are you stoked about finance? Do you love that world?" Based on her blank expression, I was afraid of what she was going to say. And sure enough: "Oh, God no. I pretty much hate it. But being an accountant is good money. And my dad wants me to do this. And he's paying my tuition." And she just shrugged, as if it all made perfect sense. I saw two things in her future: A Mercedes. And Prozac.

This may sound idealistic, romantic, and naïve. It may sound unreasonable and absurd in light of how difficult, grueling, and downright wretched being on this planet can sometimes be. But . . .

> The point of life is happiness.
>
> —The Dalai Lama

CHOOSING FULFILLMENT TURNS THE TIDE OF HISTORY

When we make feeling good a priority, everything changes—our individual lives change, and social systems change. How we make and spend money changes. How we teach and learn changes. How we love changes. Think of all the freedom fighters and activists who decided that openly loving and respecting whom they wanted to made them feel good. That feeling of liberation was more important to them than social acceptance, and it was worth the risk to fight for equal rights. Black, white, gay, straight—whoever they were, regardless of what category they fit into, their desire to be free and fulfilled revolutionized society.

Heading toward your core desired feelings will revolutionize your life.

There are feelings, and then there are *core desired* feelings.

As you use your feelings as your guidance system more and more, you might wonder about fickle feelings, fluid feelings that will change under you while you're trying to build the life you want. So how do you know that the feelings you are basing your core desired feelings on are solid, reliable ones and not the changeable, fleeting ones? I asked my very wise coach friend, Lianne Raymond, who is a psychology teacher. She responded to this beautifully by saying:

"The range of feelings we may experience throughout a day are reactive feelings—meaning they originate in our reactions to circumstances. Different circumstances arouse different feelings (getting stuck in traffic versus getting a raise at work). They change easily and frequently."

Core desired feelings are generative feelings. They originate deep within us and make themselves known when we take the time to listen. They do not change with circumstances. Jungian analyst Marion Woodman calls them "the soul cry." They are generative because they are the place from which our life becomes a creation, like an acorn on its way to becoming the oak. Grounded in our core desired feelings, we act from creative (rather than reactive) energy.

While core desired feelings don't fundamentally change, we may become more aware of their nuances and refinements as we become wiser and better listeners. In order to overcome the conditioning that has dampened our awareness of our core desired feelings, we may need to consciously invoke them through deliberate practice. But as we continue to acknowledge them and give them the space they crave, we will find ourselves coming from that place more and more spontaneously.

When we are immersed in the process of revelation while working through *The Desire Map,* it is good to remember that **the soul always desires that which will most reveal its true nature.**

When we are able to recognize our core desired feelings as sparks of divinity that can begin the illumination of our life, there is a feeling of *ahhh . . .* We are unveiling what is already there—not adding yet another layer to our already cloaked hearts. **There is a sense of having arrived home.**

GETTING TRUTHFUL

We can deceive ourselves into thinking that certain things will bring us happiness. Self-deception is part of self-discovery. Inevitably, we will do things for the wrong reasons.

Learning to stay close to our Soul is an organic process, full of missteps along the way.

Let's go back to the university student I just spoke of, who, despite loathing accounting, was going to become an accountant to please her father. She could arguably say that pleasing her dad made her "happy." And so, she "feels good" about that. But that's not whole happiness. In truth, her pursuit is driven by fear. Perhaps fear of independence, fear of disapproval, or fear of hardship.

Her focus is not on being happy. Her focus is on not being *unhappy*. There's a vast and absolute difference. (We'll explore this difference when we talk about motivation vs. inspiration.)

We can always find ways to justify our behaviors to meet soulless goals. *It was the right thing to do. It's the bottom line. I had obligations. I didn't want to hurt his feelings. There was a lot of money on the line. I was too far in. It's the way it's always been done.*

I've worked my ass off to hit targets and launch stuff that made me feel flat and less than proud. I've joylessly pursued goals that I didn't fully believe in, because I wanted to be successful. That's twisted. And it never paid off, no matter how good I looked while I was doing it, no matter how together everyone else thought I was. It cost me—big time. My definition of success needed a major overhaul.

And that's what's required for most of us when we decide that the journey matters as much as the result, and that we want to have a good time most of the time: we radically alter our personal definition of success.

FEELINGS ARE MAGNETIC

EACH FEELING IS A BEACON
THAT ATTRACTS A REALITY

LOVE ATTRACTS LOVE

GENEROSITY ELICITS
A GENEROUS RESPONSE

ANGER CREATES MORE THINGS
THAT COULD MAKE YOU EVEN ANGRIER—
IF YOU LET THEM

WHAT WE FOCUS ON EXPANDS

SO CHOOSING TO FOCUS ON LIFE-
AFFIRMING FEELINGS IS THE SUREST WAY
TO CREATE THE EXPERIENCE YOU WANT

ACCENTUATE THE POSITIVE

We're not here to invalidate or avoid the dark, negative, and uncomfortable feelings that are part of the human experience. Desire mapping is not about disassociating from the rough stuff. That would be lunacy, because rough stuff—loss, despair, illness, doubt, and tragedies—happens.

This is about being deliberate with our feelings. It's about taking radical responsibility for how you create your life, and how you respond to the people and circumstances around you. It's about choosing positivity when you could just as easily choose negativity.

Positivity blockers:

> › Overzealous competitiveness.

> › Ambivalence and indifference. When you're in touch with your truth, you can make a clear choice.

> › Scarcity mentality. There's not enough to go around: not enough money, clients, market space, recognition, opportunities.

> › Comparing yourself to others—feeling superior or inferior.

> › Jealousy to the point that you can't wish the other person well.

> › Preciousness to the point that you inconvenience others to get your needs met.

> › Anger. Anger can sometimes be useful and galvanizing and lead to more positive states of being. But most of the time, it's a bitch.

> › Worry. Trust me, it's useless.

LIFE-AFFIRMING DISCIPLINE

There is no easy walk to freedom anywhere, and many of us will have to pass through the valley of the shadow of death again and again before we reach the mountaintop of our desires.

—Nelson Mandela

Underneath it all, we are wild and we know it.

—Reggie Ray, Buddhist scholar

I once worked with an entertainment exec who prided herself on being disciplined. "I get up every morning at 6 a.m. to run," she told me over dinner. "I hate it, but it needs to be done." And she went on to explain that for Lent, she gave up swearing and hadn't cussed in four years ("Even though it would feel sooo good to just say the F-word sometimes!"). The following Lent, she swore off soda pop and hadn't had so much as a sip for three years ("Even though a Coke with these tacos would be grrreat!").

"Well, that sounds like a whole lotta fucking fun," I said to her. And then I asked the waiter to bring me a Coke.

Here's the thing: as hardwired achievement-bots, many of us subscribe to systems of success that actually become blockages to our instincts. Structures, programs, regimens—all disciplines and theories should be used to support our freedom and independent thinking, but many serve to stifle our life force instead.

That female exec wasn't very joyful. She quietly suffered from bouts of depression, and she was excruciatingly lonely. Despite being in shape, composed, and intelligent, her discipline didn't seem to be easing her very real pain.

Can we use 12-step programs or eating plans or time-management systems to happily pursue goals with Soul? Yes!

Can discipline feel joyful? Yes!

So how do you know when you're stifling yourself with structure vs. nurturing, or setting yourself free, with structure? You know because it feels good to do it, and it leads to more good feelings.

We may need some serious pep talks and accountability systems to make our dreams come true. But we don't need to bark orders at ourselves, and we shouldn't take abusive shit from leaders or coach-types in the name of overcoming our fears in order to win the race. Even if you do win, the punishment you accepted from someone else or inflicted upon yourself will weigh on your self-worth.

Even in the midst of the necessary hard work or restraint, you can access joy. It's positively-driven ass-busting. Have you ever been at the finish line of a marathon? None of those guys are happy about their blisters and burning muscles, but they're euphoric to be in the race. When we undertake to do what must be done with a full heart, that full-heartedness leads to a result we can love. The process affects the outcome.

The surest sign that you're working with the life-affirming kind of discipline, rather than the spirit-depressing kind, is that you don't complain very much about doing what it takes.

These days, I don't do anything that makes me miserable in order to fulfill a vision. (Okay, I organize receipts for taxes, but I do it while watching a movie.) Mostly, I don't have Soul-sucking chores on my plate. But in order to create what I want, when I want, I do some things that are hard to do, like heavy-lifting, stamina-requiring, need-to-take-my-blue-green-algae-vitamins-to-pull-it-off kinds of things. Like, once in a while I get up at five in the morning to write so I can stay on track with a launch date. That's hard work for someone who's been a night owl her entire life. But I'm just as stoked to write at 5 a.m. as I am at midnight. And I feel just as close to my life force meeting a crazy deadline as I do writing a short poem on a long holiday.

Life-affirming discipline doesn't take you further from your truth and joy, it brings you closer to it.

YOU ARE NOT YOUR FEELINGS

Choose a term that resonates with you: Soul, spirit, source power, Buddha nature, essence, pure energy, vortex, God, Godliness, divinity, original self, light, love. For our purposes, I'll go with Soul—with a capital S for both effect and respect.

Your Soul is everything. The "Am That I Am." Your beingness. The you that is simultaneously part of the all. The God that is aware of itself. Unfathomably, your Soul is the stuff of eternity, time without end, spanning space and dimensions. It is the Love of All Loves. It is the inextinguishable Source of Light. Your Soul is home.

Your Soul is the destination—and your feelings are the road signs directing you to it. Your feelings lead you home by giving you moment-by-moment signals.

In this conversation we need to differentiate between the feelings that you experience within your being, and your so-called feelings about external events. Your personal experiences of love, or expansion, or gratitude, or any emotion, are your feeling states.

Your thoughts or opinions about a situation are not your feeling states. Here's an example: You can watch a movie that you thought was depressing, but still feel happiness. You can interact with someone who you think is negative, and you can still experience deep joy within yourself. You can have any number of intellectual opinions about politics, and those mental perspectives are separate from the emotionality you have.

The capacity to witness something that your mind or outside sources might label as negative, and to remain in a positive feeling state while doing so, is what self-determination—and transcendence—is about. Think about people who are peaceful even in chaos, or generous when they're broke, or loving in the face of oppression. Think of Nelson Mandela experiencing inner freedom while in prison.

You can't always choose what happens to you, but you can always choose how you feel about it.

A traffic jam is a great example of how different people can choose to feel differently about the same situation. Crawling along in the commuter lane, Heather Happy is rocking out to her tunes, thinking about the project she's working on and what she'll make for dinner—and she's feeling a lot of gratitude and a goodly amount of peace. *All is well, right time, right place—this traffic jam at least gives me time to unwind.*

Driving right behind her is Debbie Downer. She's also rocking out to her tunes, thinking about the project she's working on, and what she'll make for dinner—and she's pissed off and frustrated. *Goddamn commute. Why does this always happen to me? Who's the bozo who's holding this up?*

Being able to experience peace, even appreciation, when you're in a tough situation is a result of being in touch with your Soul. The feeling of peacefulness is the indicator of who you really are. Conversely, feeling like a bag of aggravated worry balls is an indicator that you're out of touch with your greatness.

Peace or worry. Gratitude or anger. It's your choice.

FEELINGS OR EMOTIONS? JUST A SIDE NOTE.

As long as you feel inspired, your life is being well spent.

—Hugh MacLeod

We could have an unending debate about what a feeling is and what an emotion is. In fact, I asked a few thousand people on Facebook and Twitter for their opinions on the matter and it got insightfully, confusingly, entertainingly emotional—really fast. What we can agree on is that a lot of us are confused about it.

I'm taking a survey. What do you think is the difference between feelings and emotions? Discuss.

Last night in a really intense conversation I used my feelings to help me verbalize my emotions. Or at least, this is what I think I did.

Emotions are driven by the ego and feelings are driven by emotions . . . I think. :)

Emotions are short-term, feelings are long-term?

If I cut myself—feeling—I can emote about it later.

Feelings are often dictated by thoughts and are subject to constant change pending said thoughts.

Emotions come from the pit of your stomach and feelings come from your heart.

Feelings are to emotions what waves are to the ocean.

Emotions are commonly reactions to feelings . . . both of which are subject to hormones and history.

Feelings is slang for emotion.

Same thing, different words.

And my very favorite response, this weighty data from Nicholas Korn:

> The Emotions released the disco dance track "The Best of My Love"
> in 1977, while "Feelings" was released by Albert Morris in 1975.
> So the difference, I guess, would be two years.

Emotions and feelings are not the same thing. They are seemingly inextricable but they are, in fact, distinct. Like the tree and its fruit. It's problematic terrain because people—from psychologists to poets—often use the words interchangeably, with implied authority, and yet define them in widely differing ways.

I asked my favorite intuitive and metaphysician, Hiro Boga, to sum it up:

> *Feelings are direct energetic responses to experiences*—they
> are communications from your body. Our bodies respond constantly
> to what's happening in and around us. Those responses take the
> form of feelings. Feelings are specific, vibrational responses to our
> experiences.
>
> *Emotions are feelings that have a mental component added—*
> a thought, story, belief, pattern, or picture that often (though not
> always) acts as a prism through which the feeling is interpreted
> rather than simply felt. This can shape the feeling energy and freeze
> it into a rigid form. Emotions tend to be less fluid, less responsive
> to direct experience.

Based on Hiro's definitions, if we simply let ourselves feel what we're feeling, the feeling energy moves through and naturally changes—as all energy changes. Feelings are fluid.

This rings true for me, but I'll be using the two words interchangeably throughout, for the sake of both simplicity and flavor.

Here's the thing: your definition of feelings only needs to make sense to you. All we really need to agree on is that you know a positive feeling (or emotion) when you feel it. Good, bad. Happy, sad. Positive, negative. You know it.

THE BENEFIT
OF CLEAR DESIRES

What you seek is seeking you.

—Rumi

LESS PROVING, MORE LIVING

Maybe you don't need to make six figures a year. Or be married by the time you're thirty. Or be team captain. Or sit in an ashram watching your in breath and out breath. Or have a pension.

Or maybe those are *exactly* the things that you need to have and do to feel the way you want to feel.

When you get real about the feelings that you crave, you might surprise yourself with some new choices. You'll sign up for workshops you'd never considered. You'll quit stuff. You could realize that you don't need to be VP to feel powerful or useful, you just need to volunteer at the youth shelter. Maybe you don't need that award, you just need to take better care of yourself.

Clarity about your true desires is so liberating because you get to stop proving yourself to everyone (including yourself). Just think about that for a minute. *No more proving.* Do you feel giddy about that? Because I do.

I met SARK at a cocktail party. SARK is also known as Susan Ariel Rainbow Kennedy, and her posters and books, like *Succulent Wild Woman, Living Juicy,* and dozens of others, have been read by millions. She dazzles in person. I wanted to sit at her feet and hear any wisdom she wanted to give. We connected immediately. "Tell me anything!" I said. "Like, what's your thing these days? Anything." She didn't skip a beat. She looked me straight in the eye and, all sparkly but deadly serious, she said, "No striving."

I whispered it back to her, nodding my head up and down like I'd just heard the secret password of all time. "No striving." And then I upped the volume to eureka-level. "No striving! Oh my God, you have no idea how much I needed to hear this right now," I told her. We chanted it together (chant it with me now): "No striving." And we giggled like pretty witches.

Then SARK went on to tell me the fabulously unorthodox ways in which she runs her sizeable publishing empire. She told me about the flashy offers she's declined and the financially profitable projects she put an end to so that she could feel more spiritually profitable—which of course led to even more profitability. "I stopped pushing years ago. I changed my definition of success. I gotta feel juiced. Juiced is the goal."

All juice. No push. Feeling good is the goal. Check.

WITH CLEAR DESIRE, YOU CAN SAY YES TO THE RIGHT OPPORTUNITIES

What we strive for
in perfection
is not what turns us
into the lit angel
we desire,
what disturbs
and then nourishes
has everything
we need.

—David Whyte

So you're clear on how you most want to feel. Let's say, adventurous, love, energized, and prospering. Excellent. Next, you start envisioning feeling that way in your ideal relationship and details start coming to mind.

You imagine that Mr. or Miss Right is good-looking, of course; and they have a great education, like you do, so you can have an intellectual match; and they're athletic, 'cause you're a sporto and you want someone to bike with. And ideally (because we are going for ideal), they don't smoke and they love to travel, because you are ready for some adventure, baby!

And then you meet someone at a friend's BBQ, and you're completely intrigued and attracted to this person. You feel energized, like you light up a few more watts in their presence. But they're not as hot as you were hoping—a little chubby maybe. And you're taken aback to learn—after talking fluidly for hours on all of your favorite topics—that despite being a working writer, they never went to college. *Hmmm. Well that's too bad,* you think, *my brother won't be very impressed.* They're not matching up to the details of your vision. But . . . you're feeling pretty jazzed to be around them.

On your first date this paramour takes you to a poetry slam in a seedy part of town, and it opens up your world. *The passion! The politics!* Then they take you out for Ethiopian food, which you've never had before. You feel like you're on an adventure in your own city. You want more of this! You're feeling love starting to move through you. And by God, you laugh more than you've ever laughed.

And then you learn that this person, who is clearly incredibly cool and is turning you right on, is afraid of flying on planes. In fact, they have such a phobia of flying that they've never been off the continent. Errrrt! Grinding halt. What about that honeymoon in Paris you'd always dreamed of? And your friend's birthday party in Chile? No flights. A little bit chubby. No alma mater. The deal could be off.

Except . . . you feel the way you wanted to feel. Adventurous. Love. Energized. The packaging is a bit funky, but the feelings are so right. And you surprise yourself. You give in to your core desired feelings. You're a yes! Three cheers for truth! Fears silenced, heart engaged. You're not compromising. In fact, you're expanding.

You have a backyard wedding and road trip for your honeymoon. Mazel tov. And then, because this is a real love story, you promptly find a great couples therapist, who helps you conclude that going to Paris with your best friend, and coming home to a devoted partner who totally turns you on, is a pretty sweet deal.

When you're clear on how you want to feel, you can be open to what life wants to give you. And life usually has something even better in store for you than what you've imagined.

Stay anchored to the desired feeling, and open to the form in which it manifests.

DESIRE BRINGS LIGHT TO DARKNESS

Longing, felt fully, carries us to belonging.

—Tara Brach, *Radical Acceptance*

This is what I know to be true: when I'm in a hellish kind of anger or feeling painfully disconnected, I want to get out of it as fast as possible. It's taken me years to realize that tuning in to my most desired feelings—my preferred states of being—gives me some immediate relief. And more than that, it helps healing to happen.

The Situation: I'm feeling angry because something is not the way that I want it to be. My partner just did that "thing" again and I'm pissed right off. (*How many times—and ways—do I have to ask him not to do that thing!?*) Huffy huff puff. Huff. Grrrr. Puff.

The cascading effect of disparaging monkey-mind chatter:

He can be such an asshole. No . . . I'm *such an asshole for thinking* he's *such an asshole. But he's got a problem, I mean, really. If only he'd change that one thing. No, there's something wrong with* me. *If only I'd change. I need to be more loving, evolved, Buddhist, feminine, flexible, understanding, tough. This is just an old wound I'm bumping up against. This is all* my *shit. This isn't really happening in the present. Maybe I should move my therapy appointment to Monday, or read some Pema Chödrön. I need to get to yoga tonight to open my heart chakra. Think positive thoughts, Danielle, think about how awesome all this other stuff in your life is. But I'm still pissed . . .*

And the mental loop plays over and over. So then I try to pull out of it by thinking happy affirmation thoughts: I love my life (which I mostly do, but at the moment, this affirmation feels like a bullshit pick-up line). So I go down the spiral of psycho-critique and I analyze the shit out of "his issues" and "my issues." And not only does this fake cheer and intellectualization bum me out even more, it drags the conflict out even longer.

I know you know what I'm talkin' about.

The Solution: None of this chatter or analysis—whether it's true or objective or not—actually helps me to feel better in the moment. And by "feel better," I mean centered and at one with my life source. By "feel better" I do not mean right, soothed, or self-placated. I'm not interested in a Band-Aid for my pain, I'm interested in the antidote. And I'm very interested in getting that STAT. *What will take away this pain?*

In the toughest of moments, what makes me feel better is thinking about my core desired feelings.

If things are feeling constricted and downright fucking impossible, I think, *I desire light. What I really want is fluidity. I'd prefer communion.* It interrupts the mental jackhammering. And then I feel closer to home, aware again of my Soul. By reminding myself of what I really want in those moments, I haven't invalidated what's happening and I haven't taken myself future-tripping. I've just plugged into my ever-present desire. And it's surprisingly uplifting.

Recalling your desired feelings when you're not getting what you want

> › interrupts your mental complaints, and . . .

> › points you in the direction of what you do want, which . . .

> › allows for some optimism to slip into your mind, which . . .

> › gets you closer to the expanded state of "what's possible," which . . .

> › opens your heart, which . . .

> › is not only comforting, but allows the light of consciousness to enter, by which you can see more clearly.

And when the light of consciousness is helping you see more clearly, you can make more empowered choices. You can see solutions, you can find remedies to help you heal, you can feel gratitude for what's happening in the moment—and this last one alone can change everything. You can even lighten up and laugh—and stop being such an asshole.

So when you're jammed up, or feeling hopeless, or blind with rage, play the desire card: "I desire harmony." "Confidence, please." "Freedom, thank you."

It may take the universe a few hours, days, or years to deliver. More accurately, it might take you a while to be ready to allow those fulfilled desires into your life. But even in that instance, you will nonetheless have made your wishes known and created a more expanded moment.

YOU CAN MAKE YOUR LIFE BETTER. DAILY. PRACTICALLY.

A desire is anything but frivolous. It is the interface between you and that which is greater than you. No desire is meaningless or inconsequential. If it pulls you, even a little bit, it will take everyone higher. Desire is where the Divine lives, inside the inspiration of your desire. Every desire is of profound importance with huge consequences, and deserves your attention.

—Mama Gena

This is the single most practical reason to get clear on your core desires: you can make small improvements to your being and your life, on a daily basis.

You don't need to leave your job. Or learn Spanish, or a whole new meditation practice, or a seven-step system. You don't need to make a phone call to clear the air with the person who did you wrong ten years ago. You don't even need to be bold.

To feel the way you want to feel as often as possible, you just need to do easy things to help you feel that way every day.

One of my core desired feelings is "divinely feminine." But I'm not going take up belly dancing or lead goddess circles in my living room. Because, a) I'm an introvert, and b) my life is full. When I think about what I can do to generate "divinely feminine" on a day-to-day basis—among all the other things I have put on my plate—it has to be really simple and doable. And natural.

I can text my man something sweet or saucy. Last week, I decided to reread a chapter of Clarissa Pinkola Estes's *Women Who Run With the Wolves,* and I made sure to keep my tea date with my girlfriend. I bought tickets to see Alanis Morissette. One day I just Googled "divine feminine" and kept some goddess images I found on my computer for the day. On the days when I'm just not feeling very Sexy Wonder Woman Kali Mama Goddess Power Chica, divinely feminine can be as simple as opting to wear a skirt instead of yoga pants. And that small, sometimes simple, choice for feeling good can change the way I feel all day.

On one particularly broke day, I was feeling anything but affluent. Credit cards were full, rent was due, and the phone hadn't been ringing with new business that week. *What'll make me feel better off?* I thought. *What will I do when I am actually bringing in the bucks? Answer: I'll buy that Italian linen sofa at Inform!* So I headed down to that snooty furniture store in the hip part of town and I sat my ass on that sofa—for a conspicuously long time. *This is what affluence feels like—quality,* I thought. And I felt a bit better. I felt a little more possible. Which made me feel more like myself. And instead of focusing on feeling broke, I shifted my focus to going after what I wanted. It was just a small, but effective, thing to get me out of my funk and back to feeling inspired to make things happen.

Small, deliberate actions inspired by your true desires create a life you love.

When you're not feeling the way you want to feel, it can take just a small gesture to shift your state of mind. I have a friend who's a freelance writer, and she's made a habit of giving stuff away when she's feeling lacking. "I pay for dinner with a friend, even if things are tight for me, or I do some writing work pro bono. It opens my heart up, and money seems to flow better when I'm feeling more generous about life."

Immerse yourself in the energy of what you desire.

—Hiro Boga

Seek out environments that match your desired feelings. I know someone who goes to test drive new cars when she's feeling shabby. Meander around open house showings for homes that are currently out of your price range. Go to an art gallery and be in the midst of transcendent, priceless art. Let the beauty and the power rub off on you.

The idea is that you do easy, natural things that are aligned with your core desired feelings. These small, steady actions won't change your life in a flash, but they will change your life day by day.

AN IMPORTANT DISTINCTION TO MAKE

Being deliberate about how you want to feel is at the root of self-reliance, and it's also a collaborative effort you make with life. We help form our reality by projecting out our requests and hoping they'll be met. And there's a really important distinction to be made here about where we project our desires.

Are we looking to ourselves to feel the way we want to feel, or are we relying too much on others to help us feel the way we want to feel?

Let's work with the core desired feelings of "generous" and "strong" as examples. You're wishing for generosity and strength to be your regular state of mind. So it's not about your boss or your best friend being generous and strong *for* you, or their behavior *helping* you feel generous and strong. It's not about your job feeling generous and strengthening. It's about *you* being generous and strong, within that job, or within your friendship.

We're not laying our desire trip on the world. *But you don't make me feel the way I want to!* Emotional intentionality is not about manipulating the actors in your play to create the right scene. It is about improvising and getting in the right frame of mind regardless of how other people are appearing on your stage.

You can feel light when someone else is heavy. You can feel confident when things go sideways.

You can feel beautiful amidst the ugly parts of life.

Now you may be thinking, *But don't we want to attract people who are aligned with our desires? Don't we want the world around us to be a source of pleasure?*

Yes, yes, absolutely! We want the universe to deliver pleasure (and the universe is, in fact, designed to deliver pleasure straight to our door). But when we come from a place of trying to control people and circumstances to feel good, then we step outside of our true power.

Collaborate with the cosmos instead of dictating to the world. You're stronger when you stand in your own power and dance with what's around you.

RESPECT YOUR DESIRES

You're in a troubling, less-than-terrific moment and you say to yourself, "I want to feel vitality." Excellent intentionality! You're focused on your positive desire. But then you slide this in: "Because this situation is so goddamn unbearable and I can't believe I got myself into this!" Oopsie, we just took a hard left to Gloomsville and ended on a bad note. You have just turned a perfectly good wish into a bitch-slap.

Bitch if you need to. Get it out. Just don't let it end with that. Do whatever you have to do to get your thoughts back on a positive creative track so that you're in line with your Soul. This is the good, hard work of grown-up awareness.

I want to feel peace . . . but I'm enraged . . . so I must be defective . . . All that therapy and I still get stuck like this . . .

Keep going and get back on track:

. . . and I still know that what I want the most is peace.

That's it. Simple. Just put one more drop in the bucket and it can tip your energy.

If we can feel even slightly more expanded during a painful incident, then we can build our positivity muscle in that moment. And when we practice this over time, we develop the strength to turn things around more quickly, or even to resist downward spirals altogether.

DON'T JUDGE HOW YOU WANT TO FEEL

I want to be incredibly wealthy! Is that greedy?

I want to feel loved. Is that needy?

Maybe. Maybe you're being ruled by what Buddhists call "the hungry ghost." The hungry ghost is the over-needful, ravenous part of our psyche that demands to be fed—attention, gratification, comfort, whatever the hot-spot emotion is for us. It's scared, it's always empty, and it will never be pleased.

Or maybe what you label as needy or greedy is really an impulse to heal and take care of yourself. Doing what it takes to get your needs met in a healthy way is part of a maturing spirit. Self-soothing. Radical self-responsibility. Intentional creating.

Until we admit to and honor the fact that we just want to feel [you name it], we can't even begin to experience the satisfaction we crave.

The more you are judging a desired feeling, the more it's asking for your attention.

I was once in a work partnership in which I almost obsessively craved freedom. I secretly wanted my own gig and business—I wanted my own freedom. It wracked me with guilt. I told myself I was selfish. I needed to get over it. *It's just a personality flaw from being an only child.* I drove myself crazy trying to talk myself out of who I really was. When freedom finally happened and this partner and I parted ways, I felt like I'd stepped out of a movie and back into my real life. And I vowed then to put my desire for freedom at the center of everything I did.

It doesn't matter if your core desired feelings are springing forth from a place of extreme lack or from a place of great abundance. The fact is, they are your current desires and they're trying to show you something: the way to your Soul.

> Those who restrain their desire
> do so because theirs is weak enough to be restrained.
>
> —William Blake

THE WAYS IN WHICH YOU GET
YOUR NEEDS MET WILL EVOLVE

We create wellness or dysfunction in our lives by how we go about getting our needs met.

In a delusional moment you might think that going on a weekend bender or sleeping with that coworker who is only passably enticing to you is going to make you feel all free 'n' loved up. But if you're feeling guilty and ashamed while you're going for supposed fulfillment, then you're missing the mark.

If you have to step outside of yourself, away from your values and Soul, to get your needs met, then you're not really going to get your needs met. The process itself of bringing your core desired feelings to life has to be infused with the feelings you're going for. If you're aiming for big freedom this year, then do stuff that makes you feel free today.

When you come face-to-face with your burning need, when you can say to yourself with some sincere amazement, *For the love of God, do I ever crave to feel seen and connected* (for example), then you can start to relax into yourself. And in this more relaxed and accepting place, the agitated, demanding energy around the desire will start to cool down and you can think more clearly about how to get fulfilled in positive ways. You won't need to stomp your feet or have one glass of wine too many. You'll trust that you've got what it takes to create something satisfying. And you'll inch out to do it.

At first you may need someone to give you permission, some external validation. Go get it. Call your friends and ask them to tell you why you're so special. Hire a coach to cheer you on.

And then, as a next step toward good feelings, maybe you'll need to do something rather significant or dramatic. You'll know when it's time.

Stay steady with your wanting. On really hungry days you may have to whisper to yourself over and over again, *I just want to feel what I want to feel . . . I just want to feel what I want to feel . . .* reminding yourself that you always have the right to desire something more than what's currently in front of you.

Eventually, how you create your most wanted feelings will become a habit of your true nature—instinctively healthy and self-aware. You'll have worked your way up as CEO of your own fulfillment—and you will have so much to give to the world.

THE UNDENIABLY IMMENSE VALUE OF NEGATIVE EMOTIONS

In the depth of winter I finally learned
that there was in me an invincible summer.

—Albert Camus

Positive feeling states are a sign that we're in sync with our Soul.

Negative feeling states are indicators that we're out of sync with our Soul.

And we're going to get out of sync. We're going to forget about our magnificence a hundred times a day. Some people will only glimpse their own magnificence a few times in a lifetime. Crushingly, some of us will spend the majority of our adult lives in resistance to our Souls, in perpetual states of bitchdom and fearfulness. To those people I want to say: "You've simply forgotten who you are—it's just a temporary situation."

Getting off track is not only natural, but it is also absolutely inevitable for every single one of us. It doesn't matter if you're markedly wiser than the majority, if you're in beautiful, selfless service to the world, an avowed monk, or a relentless reader of self-help books with years of therapy, a yoga pass, and the aligned chakras to prove it. You're going to slip out of your Soul zone and into the shadowy emotions of doubt, jealousy, pettiness, vengefulness, and a whole cadre of other uncomfortable states of being.

Getting off track is essential to our growth.

Veering away from one's essence and steering back to it is how we accumulate insight into, and trust in, the nature of life. We learn more about both our personal and the universal landscape every time we take a wrong turn. And how do we know we've taken a wrong turn? Well, generally speaking, we feel like shit. We feel exactly how we don't want to feel.

How about reframing negative feelings as wake-up calls? I like to think of these incessant, negative, niggling emotions as regular reminders of the awesomeness that I have access to, even when I'm feeling like a total cow.

I have a quick temper and, while I'm not proud of it, I am also a semi-professional critic of just about everything. This very special combination of qualities means that Rage Lite is a regular part of my daily existence. LaPorte weighs in on poor customer service: *Are you fucking kidding me?* On yet another saccharine Hollywood movie: *Are you fucking kidding me?* On my man leaving his big damn boots right in front of the door, again: *Are you fucking kidding me?* And so it goes, my fast-track path to enlightenment.

Are my mini-geysers of frustration indicators that I'm acting from my truest nature? Nope. That frustration, which at its darkest can become contempt, is telling me that I've forgotten what I know to be true: that we're all doing our best, we're all worthy of love, and all is well. The golden luminous nature of existence does not sweat the small stuff.

Is frustration, or any other negative emotion, useful or worthwhile? Hell yes. Every emotion felt is valuable. The trick is to actually feel it—and then to fully accept it. Judging ourselves for feeling less than outstanding, or for being adrift from our divinity for a minute, or several months, only keeps us locked in those negative states. If we're condemning it, we're creating stuckness. When we wipe the residue of judgment off the lens, we can see where more positive options are waiting for us.

My Rage Lite reminds me of what I truly desire: joy. It nudges me to laugh at myself. Sometimes it reminds me that the most loving act can be to just let it go. Sometimes it spurs me to take action. My anger reminds me of peace. My sadness, of happiness. My fear, of faith.

FEELINGS MAY NOT LOOK HOW THEY FEEL

On poetry: Everyone wants to know what it means.
But nobody is asking, How does it feel?

—Mary Oliver

We can be quick to identify certain feelings as "bad" or less than ideal, and so we expend a lot of energy avoiding those feelings or judging ourselves for feeling them.

We need to keep in mind how fluid and multidimensional feelings are.

Just like an ocean can be pounding the beach with waves yet be perfectly calm at its depths, our feelings may look destructive, or inappropriate, or negative, when really they are expressions of something incredibly hopeful coming from deep within us.

So, on some days, an angry outburst might really be a wave of creative energy coursing through you. *Fight for your rights!* Or that tremor of grief could be the stirring of your most tender compassion. What looks like fear might actually be excitement. As my speaking coach, Gail Larsen, always reminds me, "Fear is excitement without the breath."

Only you can say what feels true.

NEGATIVE FEELINGS ARE STEPPING-STONES TO MORE POSITIVE FEELINGS

Every need brings what's needed.
Pain bears its cure like a child.
Having nothing produces provisions.
Ask a difficult question,
And the marvelous answer appears.

—Rumi

Restriction can lead to freedom. Shame can lead to pride. Weakness can lead to integrity. But you need to stay in motion in order to get from one state to the next, constantly referring to your inner GPS of feelings. "Right now I'm traveling south on Despair Highway, which means I'm about nine hundred miles away from Joy. I better take the off ramp to Courage." And pretty soon, possibly in an instant, you'll be right where you want to be.

Abraham-Hicks, creators of books like *Ask and It Is Given* and *The Astonishing Power of Emotions,* have a theory about manifesting what you want that they call "rockets of desire."

The idea is that every conscious desire you have gets projected out into the cosmos like a rocket, and the universe is collecting your wishes until you're ready to have them fulfilled. I love this notion. But here's where it gets even more compelling: you also send out a rocket of desire every time you experience something that you do *not want.* An unwanted occurrence happens, and then you consciously—or unconsciously—desire something better, and zoom, out goes another rocket of desire requesting that something better occur for you.

This is a spectacular theory—it's so liberating. It means that all experience is useful, that everything is progress. Bearing that in mind can be profoundly comforting when things are falling apart. So consider this: every unwanted emotion and experience you encounter is a wish for something better, and that wish is being heard. Keep wishing, wanting, and aiming. You're getting closer to true joy with every desire.

WHY DO WE PUSH AWAY GOOD FEELINGS?

> Our species in general had grown accustomed to pain and adversity
> through millennia of struggle. . . . We were only recently evolving
> the ability to let ourselves feel good and have things go well
> for any significant period of time.
>
> —Gay Hendricks, *The Big Leap*

Because we don't feel worthy. Because we're focused on pleasing others instead of ourselves. Because we want to be loved. Because we're trying to win at someone else's reward system. Because we're told not to get too big for our britches. Because we're operating on the premise that what other people think actually matters to our well-being.

Because it feels vulnerable to feel good, and we start to fear that it won't last. Because positive feelings such as joy, happiness, bliss, abundance, and more, are very very powerful. And that kind of energy current can shake up our emotional structures—joy can blow your mind. Positive emotions can also be threatening to the people around us who'd prefer miserable company.

Joy does not fit into the box of the status quo.

Unfetter your happiness (you know you want to).

How are things? *Good. Yeah, good. Fine. Things are fine.*

Let me ask that question again: How are things?

Fabulous! It all feels like an adventure right now. I have synchronicities piling up everywhere. I've got all the money I need, in fact, it's flowing good 'n' steady. My skin is glowing. Most nights we dance in the kitchen. Sex is good. I giggle every day. And really, sometimes when I smile at a stranger in the market I can feel my heart swell. In fact, I swear I felt bliss while I was walking home the other day from the market. Yeah. It was bliss.

Happy? Then say so.

I notice this in myself, and I see it in other people: the happiness muffle. We feel the sparkle; really we do. We feel rich with gratitude, and we're even keenly aware of a true smile curled up in our cells. But even if we truly tend to live on the light side of things, we don't pronounce it. As coach Lianne Raymond puts it, "We butt back the joy because happiness is a form of power."

Is that any way to treat happiness? Happiness is power. Happiness is carbonated consciousness. It wants to spill out and radiate and be articulated. And every time we downplay our joy we confuse our synapses. Our brain is firing smiley neurons and our mouth is short-circuiting them. Happiness-muffling numbs our senses. If you keep it under the surface too long, it just might stay there—a light under a bushel.

Admit to your contentment so it can grow.

KNOWING HOW WE FEEL

Birds flying high you know how I feel
Sun in the sky you know how I feel

—as sung by Nina Simone

I was walking with a friend in a field of tall grass on a perfect summer day. It was completely idyllic. There was even a babbling brook. *Cotton is high and I'm feeling fine,* I thought to myself.

My friend had just gone off antidepressants and antianxiety meds after five-plus years of off-and-on. She was having a hard time managing her feelings at this point, mostly because she hadn't felt them in so long—they confused her. "So how are you feeling these days?" I asked her. "I just don't know. I think I feel things, but I'm not sure what to call them. I don't know if this is anger or sadness, or if I'm feeling happiness or just *wanting* to feel happy." We just walked in silence, peacefully, for a lot of that afternoon.

After you've been numbed for a while, disorientation is a natural reaction as you come back around. It's like waking up from anesthesia and not knowing exactly where you are.

We all numb out to some degree—avoiding the negative feelings that are painful and seemingly impossible to transmute, or deflecting the positive feelings that seem foreign to our system and threatening to our habitual ways of being. We down the wine, light up, sugar out. We gorge on TV, distract ourselves with shopping, snack on gossip, let our minds natter on.

But when we avoid the greater range and depths of feelings over the long term it makes for shallow and narrow living—actually, it makes for not quite living at all. So upping our willingness to feel the full range of our feelings is a surer way to create healing.

FOR THE
FULL RANGE
OF HUMAN
EMOTION

That doesn't mean that we act out the dark emotions. To the contrary, one of the reasons to be aware of all of our feelings is so that we can be deliberate about the emotions that we play out in the world and in our work.

We need to honor the diversity of our emotions, respect all of our faces, masks, and sounds—even the dark stuff. *Ah, rage, there you are yet again, teaching me about peace.*

When you can respect the darkness within yourself without any guilt trips, you're becoming truly free.

> But if in your fear you would seek only love's peace and love's
> pleasure, then it is better for you that you cover your nakedness
> and pass out of love's threshing-floor, into the seasonless world
> where you shall laugh, but not all of your laughter,
> and weep, but not all of your tears.
>
> —Khalil Gibran

WE'RE ALL IN THIS TOGETHER

Sometimes we need to learn to feel again. This is like relearning a dance move you haven't done for years, or getting back into the foreign language you haven't spoken since high school. After a broken heart, a long, time-enduring compromise, or years of consuming any and all kinds of feeling-blockers, it's time to take a refresher course in the geometry of feelings.

Strangely enough, even though feelings are such a preciously private experience, we can relearn how to feel somewhat by observing other people. For this reason, we need to become inspectors of the heart. Just like we check out what people are wearing, we need to become keener at checking out what they're feeling—and asking them about it. *Where'd you get that happiness? It goes great with your eyes. Are you feeling angry or sad, or is this facial expression just a habit? How come you're in such a good mood?*

There's a technique taught in acting classes for getting in touch with your own emotions as well as developing empathy for others' emotions. When you're among other people and observing them, especially strangers, you use your skills of observation to take in what you see and hear, very specifically, and then use your imagination to make stuff up about who the strangers are and what they want, what they're feeling, where they may be going.

> The great gift of human beings is that we have the power of empathy.
>
> —Meryl Streep

Sinead O'Connor taught me how to be constructively angry. The PNE Coliseum. Toronto. 1994. Acoustic encore. Only her onstage. White tank, mini kilt, army boots. "This is the last day of our acquaintance . . . I will meet you later in somebody's office." Ever so soft and sincere. And then wail, wallop, wazam! "I'll talk but you won't listen to meeeeeee!" She wailed. She made her final, cracking guitar strum, slammed the guitar down, and just as lithely as she'd entered, left the stage. The audience stared in silence at the empty spotlight. And then, the crowd went wild.

I'd never seen a woman channel rage in such a clean way. *Anger trips your freedom circuits,* I thought. That night, I decided to quit my job.

A stranger in a bar taught me about crippling depression. "When I was standing upright, the distance between the floor and me felt too far," she told me. "So I decided it was better if I just crawled around the house. I was glad we had carpeting." At the time we met she was a high-functioning, radiant woman. I've recalled her story in my own dark nights. *Radiance will happen again, radiance will happen again.*

In an interview with Oprah, Goldie Hawn said that she was so happy all the damn time because she "decided to be." When I heard this, I decided to make the same decision daily.

Seek out grand expressions of life force everywhere. When you're just waking up to the deliberate practice of feeling more in your life, it's helpful to look for outpourings of emotion in art: The agony of Edvard Munch's *The Scream.* The pride of Georgia O'Keefe's black-purple flower petals. Pablo Neruda's love poems. Beethoven's "Ode To Joy." Heart-crackers, all of them.

Be curious. Come to life.

150+ POSITIVE FEELINGS

abundant, abundance

accepting, acceptance

accessible

accomplishment, accomplished

acknowledged, acknowledgment

adorable, adored, adoring, adoration

adventure, adventurous,
  adventuresome

anticipation, anticipatory, anticipating

affectionate, affection

affluent, affluence

alive, aliveness

alluring, allure, allurement

amazing, amazement, amazed

amorous, amour

appreciation, appreciated, appreciative

at ease

attractive, attracted

authentic, authenticity

awed, awesome, in awe

balance, balanced

beatific

blessed, blessing

bold, boldness

bountiful, bounty, bounteous

boundless, boundlessness

brave, bravery

bright, brightened

brilliant, brilliance

calm, calming, calmed

capable

celebration, celebratory, celebrated

centered, centering

certain, certainty

cheerful, cheer, cheery

cherishing, cherished

clear, clarity

close, closeness

comfortable, comfort, comforted,
  comforting

confident, confidence, confiding

connected, connection, connectedness

considerate

content, contented, contentedness

courageous, courage

cozy, coziness

creative, creativity, creating

curious, curiosity

current

daring

decisive, decisiveness

delighted, delight, delightful

desired, desire, desiring, desirous

determined, determination

devoted, devotion

drawn toward, drawing toward

dynamic, dynamism

eager, eagerness

earnest, earnestness

easy, ease

ebullient

ecstatic, ecstasy

effectual, effective, effectiveness

elated, elation

elegant, elegance

embodied, embodying

emboldened

empowered, empowering

enamored

encouraged, encouraging,
  encouragement
energized, energy, energetic
enjoying, enjoyed
enlightened, enlightenment,
  enlightening
enthusiasm, enthusiastic, enthused
equanimity
excitement, exciting, excited
exquisite
fabulous, fabulosity, fabulousness
fantastic, fantasy, fantastical
fascination, fascinating, fascinated
feminine, femininity
festive
focus, focused
fortune, fortunate
free, freedom, freeing
fresh, freshness, freshened
friendly, friendship
full, fulfilled, fulfillment, fullness
generous, generosity
gentle, gentleness
genuine, genuineness
glad, gladdening, gladdened
glamorous, glamour
grace, graceful, gracious, graced
grateful, gratitude
grounded, grounding
guidance, guided, guiding
happy, happiness
harmony, harmonious, harmonic
healthy, healing, healed, health
held
home, at home, homey

hopeful, hope, hoping
holy, holiness
illuminated, illuminating, illumination
impassioned
important, importance
innovative, innovation, innovating
inquisitive
inspired, inspiration, inspiring
integrity, integrous, integral
intent, intentional, intention
interested, interest, interesting
intrigued, intrigue, intriguing
inspiration, inspiring, inspired
invigorate, invigorated, invigoration
joy, joyous, joyful
jubilant, jubilation, jubilance
keen
kind, kindness
liberation, liberated, liberal
light, lightness, lit up, lightening,
  lightened
limitless, unlimited
love, loving, loved, in love, lovely
luminous, luminosity, luminescence
magic, magical
mindful, mindfulness
masculine, masculinity
momentum
natural, nature
new, anew
nourished, nourishing, nourishment
nurtured, nurturing, nurturance
one, oneness
open, openness
open-hearted, open-heartedness

open-minded, open-mindedness

optimistic, optimism, optimist

opulent, opulence

overjoyed

passion, passionate

peace, peaceful, peacefulness

play, playful, playing

pleasure, pleasureful, pleasurable, pleasured

pleasant

positive, positivity

power, powerful

prosperity, prosperous, prospering

proud, sense of pride

purpose, purposeful, on purpose

quiet, quietude

ready, readiness

receptive, reception, receptivity, received, receiving

refreshed, refreshing, refreshment

regal, regality, regally

relaxation, relaxed, relaxing

reliable

renewed, renewal

rested, restful

revitalized, revitalizing, revitalization

rich, riches, richness

righteous, righteousness

romantic, romance, romanced

rooted, roots, rootedness

sacred, sacredness

safe, safety

satisfaction, satisfied, satisfying

secure, security

seen, seeing

sensitive

sensuous, sensual, sensitivity, sensitized, sensuality

serene, serenity

settled, settling

sexy, sexual, sexiness, sexuality

sincere, sincerity, sincereness

spontaneous, spontaneity

solid, solidity

spirit, spirited, spiritual, spirituality

strong, strength, strengthening, strengthened

supportive, support, supported

sure, surety

sweet, sweetness

tenacity, tenacious

tender, tenderness

thankful, thankfulness, thanked

thrilling, thrilled

touched, touch

treasuring, treasured, treasure

understanding, understood

unity, unified, unifying, unification, union

unique, uniqueness

useful, usefulness

value, valuable, valuing

vibrant, vibrancy

vibration, vibrating

vivacious, vivacity

vital, vitality, vitalizing

vulnerable, vulnerability

warm, warmth, warmed, warming

wealth, wealthy

whole, wholesome, holistic, wholeness

wonder, wondrous, wonderful

INTENTIONS
& GOALS

Subliminal message: Feeling good is the primary intention.

GOALS WITH SOUL?

To live in an evolutionary spirit means to engage with full ambition and without any reserve in the structure of the present, and yet to let go and flow into a new structure when the right time has come.

—Erich Jantsch

The term *goal* has many interpretations and elicits widely varied reactions—as you're about to see.

I polled the galaxy: ***Tell me, how do you feel about setting goals?***

And here's what some of you incredible earthlings had to say:

I am constantly writing down my goals, but I'm not so great at making a plan to fulfill them.

I forget about it if I get stuck, but I keep going if my desire is great enough.

Goal-setting fuckin' sucks.

Good but a little intimidated!

It can be quite frightening to set goals at times, as there is that "c" word that comes into play (gulp, commitment!!).

Love to set goals. Love achievement of goals more. I feel empowered and ignited when I set goals. They energize and invigorate me!

Confused.

I love them when they're MEGA, bold, and have IMMEDIATE consequences. (i.e., If I do not finish the rest of my certification by tomorrow (even if I have to stay up all night) I will throw the towel in on my coaching biz, completely.) (Because I've been procrastinating for a month and I'm totally capable so fuggin' do it already!) I also like when they're small and consistent, i.e., thirty days of waking up for the sunrise.

The vision is the most important part. How you get there to a lesser extent, but goals set out a path. Alter course along the way if need be, but don't lose sight of the vision.

I love setting goals, but the follow-thru is a sticky wicket . . .

I find goal setting inspiring. The thought of what I can create fuels power and momentum, and the plan creates action.

The trick is to have a timeline—transforms dreams into goals and goals into reality, from my experience.

I love GOALS!

Energized.

Great, as long as I am prepared to achieve those goals and know how I want to feel leading up to and completing each goal.

Terrified.

Setting goals is awesome; working to achieve them is a different story!

Dislike but framing them as vision and desires feels good and then stating in the freedom of the present.

I like being in the three percent of the population who does it and works toward them.

Goals are like landmarks to me—identifying them sets me on the right path, and while I may not reach every single one, just being able to see them on the horizon and in the general landscape of my journey keeps me in line and progressing.

I loathe it. It just doesn't happen.

Feels like a "have to" burden so I stopped and freedom reigned. I prefer to hold a vision and move in alignment with that.

Goals are theoretical, habits are actual—the more reliable payoff is in the latter.

Bored.

Ambivalent. While a necessary structure, I've seen so many people turn their "goal achieving" into control-freakness . . . Does "smell the roses" count as a goal?

If I don't have goals I feel lost. I'm happy for goals to be modified or even abandoned as my life changes but I like having a direction and something to focus on.

I ♥ it! Reaching them however is . . . what I delegate to the universe.

I'm just not interested in achieving anything anymore. I don't feel it's worthwhile; it's always linked to a sense that I have to become someone. I've had enough.

Like it's potentially limiting. If I am with myself, completely, then I am doing exactly what I want to be doing, which is the best thing I could do for the fulfillment of my potential. That's been a doozy to lean into, and so, so liberating.

Claustrophobic.

I have come to the conclusion lately . . . which has literally changed my life . . . and that is . . . IT IS NEVER ABOUT THE GOAL.

Blech! Phooey! I'd rather have a root canal.

Goal is too squishy. Objectives require me to think and to write in terms of specific, measurable results that I want by a specific date at a "not to exceed" cost. Not very romantic. Not at all sexy. And often they kick my butt.

It's easier since I started setting qualitative goals rather than quantitative.

Goals feel a bit like to-do lists. I instinctively wriggle in resistance even though I make them!

I love it. I set five goals per day and so does my accountability partner. We email our goals the night before, then the next evening check in with each other to ensure we both followed through. Our daily goals are designed to move us toward our weekly, monthly, and yearly goals.

Yuck. I hate them—doesn't mean I don't set them, though. I try to keep an open mind about them so that if something really incredible changes the game completely, I'm not stuck in a goal that no longer applies. I'm much more of a fly-by-the-seat-of-my-pants kind of lady.

Love goal setting. Keeps me sane—conscious creation! I set daily goals every morning, weekly goals, monthly, yearly, etc. I guess I am crazy.

Must figure out how to combine yin and yang energy of intentional thoughts/goal setting . . . THAT will kick ass!

Glad I asked.

HOW I RELATE TO GOALS

I need my conscience to keep watch over me
To protect me from myself
So I can wear honesty like a crown on my head
When I walk into the promised land.

—Dead Can Dance, "American Dreaming"

To me, setting goals feels slightly absurd, sort of inspiring, not-quite-right, and possibly awesome—all at once. Here's a commonly understood definition: "A goal is something you want in a certain way and by a certain time." Hmmm . . . I can't think of much that I've gotten in the certain way, at the certain time, that I wanted to.

I've created many things that I'm proud of. I feel deep joy on a regular basis. You could easily classify me as ambitious, but . . . I've rarely reached my "goals." **I've flat-out failed** at a lot of them—did not even come close to reaching my targeted numbers, or landing that career-changing opportunity, or getting that particular relationship on track.

Or, along the way to my destination, I did a complete **midcourse correction** and traded in my original goal for something much more fulfilling. *Changed my mind, I want* that *instead*.

Sometimes, I reached a goal waaay **later than planned,** and even though I attained it, I felt like a loser for taking so long to make it happen. (I generally feel five to ten years behind on my major life aspirations. Everything that I'm accomplishing now, well, I figure I should have nailed it by thirty-one.)

And then there were those transcendent occasions where I managed to **superexceed** my goals, in which case I felt like an idiot for thinking so small in the first place. *Should have asked for more.*

Maybe my ambivalence toward goal setting is a personality thing. Even though I want a lot out of life and my career, I'm actually not very competitive by nature. I lean toward trusting that everything happens for a reason, and I don't believe in destiny—anything could happen. Maybe it's part of being an artiste, or a Gemini, or Canadian. Or maybe goal setting is just an evil mental construct devised by The Masons to ensure the survival of industrialized nations. Yah, *that's* it.

After enough failure, rerouting, and pleasant victories, I finally considered the possibility that my resistance to goal setting wasn't out of fear, or laziness, or small-mindedness (I've got plenty of faults, but those aren't among the big ones). It's what goal chasing brought out in me that wasn't working. I was going after things—awards, privileges, numbers—to prove myself, and going about it in a way that was pushy. Proving and pushy—two surefire ways to get out of my Soul zone.

You need to have Soul-centered goals. You need to go about fulfilling those goals in life-affirming ways.

Subliminal message: Feeling good is the primary intention.

A desire presupposes the possibility of action to achieve it; action presupposes a goal that is worth achieving.

—Ayn Rand

PRESENTLY, I DON'T HAVE FIXED GOALS.

Rather, I have things that I'd really love to have happen. I have desires. And I have intentions to fulfill those desires. But I've almost fully retired from chasing things. Let me explain.

For starters, I don't run my business according to measurable objectives. We don't have targets that we work toward. There are a lot of things that I could be quantifying and pointing my efforts toward. Like the number of subscribers to my website. Books sold. Facebook fans. Quarterly revenue. All of these numbers directly impact my bottom line—and, for that matter, my happiness. But they don't guide the ship. What guides my ship is a singular, foundational intention: making stuff that feels good to make.

Unequivocally, I want to sell a lot of stuff. I'm a dyed-in-the-wool entrepreneur. I want to be immensely useful. I want to be respected and visible. And I want to be a healthy kind of wealthy. But those are the fantastic results of staying focused on my reason for being. If I lose hold of the meaningfulness, then it all becomes a lackluster grind.

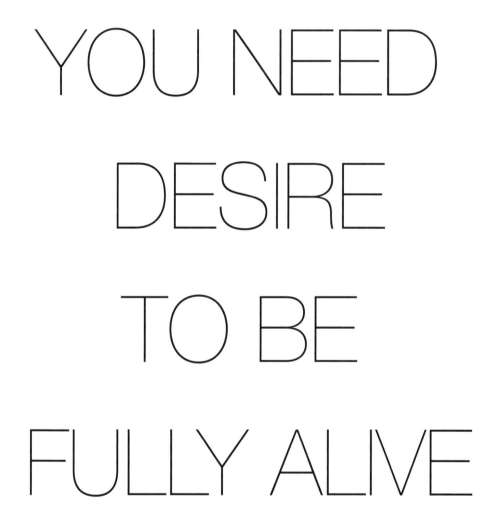

Here's what I've learned, the unavoidable hard way:

I ONLY WANT TO HIT MY TARGETS
IF THE AIMING AND THE HITTING BOTH FEEL GOOD.

And lo! The more I feel good . . . the more I feel good, which has a few incredible positive consequences: If I don't get what I wished for, I'm still in a good mood, or at least I can recover from the disappointment faster. And, because the universe is such a magnanimous and generous place, the better I feel on the way to my achievements, the more successful I am on the material plane. It's this simple: The freer I feel, and the happier I am, the more I have to give, the more I sell, the more I save, and the more doors open up.

Feeling good increases your flexibility, resiliency, effectiveness, and magnetism.

Feeling good along the way doesn't mean you don't work your ass off to get what you want. It means you *joyously* work your ass off. You don't gripe about what it takes to make things happen. You do the work. And sometimes that work is terrifying and trying and even grueling. Cycling in the pouring rain. Late-night rewrites. Struggling to open your heart after you've slammed it shut. Honoring your word when it'd be more convenient to change your mind. When you're connected to the greater purpose of an intention—honoring the call of your heart, not just proving yourself—and there's pleasure in the process, you can pull off some amazing feats.

If you're miserable when you hit your target, then it's not really a victory. If I have to dumb down, tone it down, or amp it up to be more appealing to more people, then I'm not interested. I want to be thrilled. I want love to sit at the center of my business plan, at the center of my *life*. And that's what keeps me, well, centered.

I want to feel good more than I want to check accomplishments off my list.

I want to feel good more than I want to please other people.

I want to feel good more than I want to look good.

All the goal setting I used to do, partly out of wanting to feel like a cool entre-preneur, was pecking away at my peace of mind and contributing to my already deeply entrenched complex of never being enough: big enough, loving enough, wealthy enough, strategic enough, evolved enough, popular enough.

Enough.

> A goal is not always meant to be reached, it often serves simply as something to aim at.
>
> —Bruce Lee

SOULFUL GOALS TAKE SOME PRACTICE

Before I joined creative forces with Sounds True, the publisher of this edition of *The Desire Map,* I self-published my own print version. It arrived at my house from the printer just in time for Christmas, which is usually the time of the year when I start a fresh desire map and do my intention setting. For years, I'd been doing the process by memory in my journal and now, I finally had a bonafide, for-real desire map book in my hands. I thought, *This must be how an architect feels when she walks into a building that she designed.* It was surreal.

Taking my own medicine. Jump cut to my process: I get to the "Intentions" section of *The Desire Map Workbook.* With my core desired feelings in mind, I inked out some goals for the New Year: *Make a million on this; land a deal for that; launch this big thing by a quickly approaching date.* I made a list of big, fat, specific achievables.

And then I promptly felt rather stressed. I know this feeling too well—it's the grip of goal fixation. (The very feeling that I'm trying to help thousands of people move away from.) I slipped off my own track. I had gone into default mode of setting *fixed goals,* and I had weighted my goal list with *career-based objectives.* Doh.

Curled up in bed with Egyptian chai tea and my very own Desire Map book, I just laughed out loud at myself. I had missed the whole effing, gorgeous point of desire mapping. Which is this: to go after your intentions in ways that reflect your core desired feelings—Soul-affirming, not Soul-sucking. The goal-getting itself has to feel the way you most want to feel.

Constant racing for success creates habitual and unconscious goal-setting. We need to re-learn how to move toward our dreams—with the trust and well-placed devotion.

Jump cut to my Soul groove. The goal of, "Make X dollars on X project" shifted to, "Get the message out to as many people as possible. Create liberation." "Launch project Y by Spring" turned into, "Make project Y incredibly beautiful. Launch when it feels ready." No dates. No numbers. No status. I took my career intentions for the year and put them below the intentions I set for my inner growth and relationships.

My shoulders glided down. My overheated brain felt spritzed. I felt *softer*. I felt my trust in life reentering me. Trust is crucial to creating goals with Soul. Without numbers and targets to hold on to, your heart becomes the pilot—which is the whole point, of course.

LIBERATING CHOICES

When I was still inclined to set quantifiable goals, like, "Land ten speaking gigs this year," or, "Secure a new book deal," or, "Hit 100,000 subscribers," and I simultaneously began to deepen my commitment to my core desired feelings, then I had to learn the value of saying "No, thank you" to some opportunities. As my friend Marie Forleo puts it, I got on the No Train.

Committing to feeling good above all meant that I had to pass up some things that could have helped me reach the goals I set. For example, a potential speaking gig would come along. (*Goal reminder to myself: ten gigs this year, you can do it!*) But it didn't feel quite right for one reason or another, so then I'd be forced to choose between feeling good or failing at my goal. That's a tough call to make when you're committed to happiness *and* achievement.

Choosing what felt good over the fixed goal always worked out in my favor. The lost income from the gig I passed up found another way to me. The week I would have been at the speaking event would turn out to be the same week I would later get invited on a great trip with friends. And wouldn't you know it, whenever I chose hitting the goal over a sense of ease—when I took the gig, delayed flights and crappy hotel rooms had a way of letting me know what was really best for me.

Letting go of fixed goals also helped me let go of old perceptions about what was indeed "best for me." I said yes to things that seemed out of character for a big dreamer like myself. It became less about the money and more about how spiritually fulfilling the project would be. I broke my own rules. I worked with people in different industries I hadn't considered before. I swallowed my pride and helped out where help was needed. I learned to truly embrace the belief that everything would work out if I followed the wisdom of my heart.

The more I chose my core desired feelings over my external objectives, the more content I became. In fact, those choices that seemed so tough to make at the time (*I need the money, it would be great exposure, they'll talk shit about me if I decline*) helped me surpass contentment and move into feeling liberated and creatively charged up.

I became goalless and more soulful. And all the outside things that I wanted to grow either grew (some more slowly, some more awesomely fast) or died off and made way for better things to show up. And isn't that just the natural rhythm of life? *Growth, death. It will, or it won't. 50/50. Who's to say? Anything could happen.*

The more honest I got with myself about what I was longing for, the less necessary goals seemed. So I don't have hard goals anymore—at least not the kind you can quantify. I do however have **all-consuming desires and intentions that drive me daily**—all of which are aligned with my core desired feelings.

And . . . I focus on those well-aligned intentions like I'm on fire. We'll get to that in a minute.

Subliminal message: Feeling good is the primary intention.

CHOOSE YOUR WORDS

Vision, mission, wishes, aims, objectives, aspirations, intentions, goals.

Choose a term that has a gravitational pull for you without weighing you down.

Part of a healthy relationship to material attainment and external pursuits is the language that you give it. So I choose to call it "intentions" rather than "goals." "Intention" feels like it's inwardly motivated. It feels more empowering than "vision." It also feels appropriate to use in both the context of creating feelings *and* the context of getting what you want from the world. *I intend to be joyful. I intend to trek Machu Picchu. I intend to be rapturously in love. I intend to quit this year.* Intention works—so to speak.

For the purposes of *The Desire Map,* I'm going to use the phrase "Intentions and Goals." I hope that scope makes it relatable for all of us.

But even though the language is important, I'm not, ultimately, as interested in the terminology around getting stuff accomplished as I am in the energy of how we go about accomplishing it. Have goals. Have objectives. Have intentions. Measure whatever you want, with whatever you want to call it, however you want to measure it.

Just be in *right relationship* with getting what you want. And by right relationship, I mean a relationship that feels really good to be in most of the time.

Subliminal message: Feeling good is the primary intention.

THE SPECTACULAR BEAUTY OF INTENTIONS AND GOALS

Intentions and goals sustain the human spirit.

> Without vision, we perish.
>
> —Proverbs

Intentions and goals give you clarity, and clarity gives you peace of mind.

I had no idea, but I realized that probably thirty to forty percent
of my brainpower was taken up with the questions that I couldn't
answer—because I had no direction. When I got clear on exactly
where I wanted to go, and set the goals to get there,
my mind calmed down.

—Chip Wilson, founder of lululemon

Intentions and goals bring people together.

You can have everything in life you want
if you will just help enough other people get what they want.

—Zig Ziglar

**The very act of pursuing intentions and goals—whether you manifest
them or not—helps you to know, and transform, yourself.**

Set a goal, and in small, consistent steps, work to reach it.
Get support from your peers when you start flagging. Repeat.
You will change.

—Seth Godin

Intentions and goal-setting work to help you get stuff done.

1. Goals direct attention and effort toward goal-relevant activities
and away from goal-irrelevant activities.
2. Goals have an energizing function. Goals create efforts.
3. Goals affect persistence. Goals prolong effort.
4. Goals rally us to bring task-relevant knowledge
and strategies to the problem at hand.

—Edwin Locke and Gary Latham

**Fulfilling your intentions and goals feels pleasurable, rewarding, encour-
aging, sexy, strengthening, regenerating, supportive, illuminating, wonderful, delightful, empowering, and generally fanfuckingtastic.**

Subliminal message: Feeling good is the primary intention.

ALWAYS WANTING MORE?
THE UPSIDE OF BEING INSATIABLE.

You will meet the mate of your dreams. You will hit your sales targets. You will get the gig.

And . . . you will want more. Deeper love. Greater profit. Further reach. Always wanting more.

And you will get it.

And then . . . you will want more! The new experience, the higher high, the next idea, the twist, the challenge. More. Wanting more does not make you needy or unpleaseable. (Well maybe you are, but I'm here to speak to your whole Soul.) You're not vacuous, or rapacious, or overly greedy. You're a Creator.

If you're on your creative edge, you will continuously want more. True desire is full . . . and insatiable. She is appreciative and ceaseless. She is present and she sees possibility everywhere. This is the divine paradox of intentional creating: You will love what you've got with all your heart today, and you will be ready for more tomorrow. And the next day.

THE PROBLEM WITH RIGID
GOAL CHASING

Intentions and goals are tools for liberation. But when we use goal chasing like a hammer, it can beat up on our self-esteem, relationships, and creativity.

If you're going to set "goals to die by," then, well, God bless ya. Because you're setting yourself up to soldier on and trample over spirits to get what you want.

Shouting goals at yourself deafens your truth.

Misplaced determination drowns out critical signals—from your instincts, or from the people around you who can see more objectively. If you plod on no matter what, warnings that it's time to take care of yourself or change direction can go totally unheard until the blare of frustration or fatigue gets your attention.

Chasing meaningless goals will exhaust you. When we zealously go after dreams that don't nourish our spirits, we're headed straight for trouble. Anxiety disorders, betrayals, blindsiding break-ups. Goals with Soul will energize you, and when you're on track moving toward such goals, Life will keep throwing synchronicities your way.

The ego loves goals like a food addict loves sugar. Lofty goals pump up our self-image. Big goals can make us feel bigger than, or even superior to, others. My goal is better than your goal. But just as you are not your emotions, neither are you your goals. Goals can define the trajectory of your life, but they are not a reflection of your value as a human being.

Strict goals are a win/lose equation. They're awesome when you win, but they can devastate you when you lose.

Goals can perpetuate overplanning, and overplanning kills magic and possibilities.

Subliminal message: Feeling good is the primary intention.

CREATING A HEALTHY RELATIONSHIP WITH INTENTIONS & GOALS

The foundation of a good relationship with intentions and goals is keeping in mind that the primary aim of setting and working toward them is to feel the way you want to feel.

The external things we want to have, do, and experience are secondary goals, all of which get back to the whole cosmic point: experiencing your core desired feelings.

DON'T CRITICIZE WHAT YOU WANT

> When the resistance is gone, so are the demons.
>
> —Pema Chödrön

Simplicity or grandeur. Quiet or bold. As long as what you're going after conjures your most desired feelings and is a gratifying process, then you're on track with your inner truth.

Soulful intentions and goals aren't about austerity or wanting less. You don't need to aim to save the planet or sell your worldly possessions to be in your Soul zone. But hey, if downsizing makes you feel expanded, then do it!

And conversely, going after mogul-level status or fame might not be any less Soulful for you than wanting to rescue people or start a charity. If fame and fortune are what floats your boat, then climb in.

There's also a point to be made here about judging other people's goals. I'm working on this one myself in terms of compassion and tolerance. Here's what I figure: you just never can know the machinations of someone else's Soul—their karma, their dharma, their story. Maybe they're learning precisely what they need to learn in this lifetime to become self-actualized; maybe they're struggling to get free; maybe they're an enlightened being who's come to stir shit up so we can learn compassion. Life only knows.

Back to you.

If you want enlightenment and a BMW, they're yours for the wanting. A lover who ravishes you. Your own space to make art. A secure job. An Academy Award. A new bike. Tuition paid for. Economical housing. To revolutionize health care. Organic food. A year off to travel and a true friend to take the trip with you. A reliable car. A pet. A million bucks, net. Hardwood floors. Whiter teeth. To forgive. To lead a nation. To leave the house every day feeling like you have something to give the world.

Want what feels good to want.

Subliminal message: Feeling good is the primary intention.

KNOW THE COST OF HAVING IT ALL

Men are not free when they're doing just what they like.
Men are only free when they're doing what the deepest self likes.
And there is getting down to the deepest self! It takes some diving.

—D. H. Lawrence

Can we please bust the "having it all" illusion? "Having it all" is someone else's definition of success.

Do you even need it all? What if just some of it is plenty? What if your idea of bliss doesn't include the traditional components of "it all"? For instance, maybe you don't need a man or woman to feel fulfilled and instead you actually cherish being single. Your picture-perfect life has nothing to do with the suburbs, or monogamy, or having gravity-defying boobs. You're happy renting. You're happy having a boss who does the scheduling. You have no compulsion whatsoever to make more money than you need for modest living and a monthly budget for new books.

The having-it-all notion leaves a lot of us on the fringes because we don't want what we're "supposed to want." (Though, to be fair, many of us who don't actually want what we're "supposed to want" are, in fact, fringier types who are therefore usually happy on the fringe.) It can also be really detrimental to people who swim in the mainstream, but would actually like to veer off course—like the single mom in the 'burbs who'd like to date her best friend: Sally.

The having-it-all pressure can drive you crazy when things aren't so perfect. Like it did for Missy, who told me, "Hell, I had it all, on the outside. My business took off, my husband's a great guy, I had two perfect toddlers. I even had the marble kitchen countertops. But I was boozing it up in the pantry every afternoon because the pressure to be perfect was getting to me." She went on: "Ya know, sometimes I wanted to show up at our mommy walks without a great attitude, or without my makeup, and with my filthy kid, and just say, 'Ladies, this is all I fuckin' got to give today!'"

Missy had a breakdown that turned out to be a breakthrough. She then moved her family to the country, doubled her business, and quadrupled her peace of mind.

ALL THAT GLITTERS

I've had some opportunities to create my own TV show. I always felt ambivalent about it, even though it made good career sense to go for TV. I love mass communication and broadcasting my shizzle. And hey, I have a closet full of killer shoes—I "should" want a show. So I went after it. A TV producer was trying to sell me on the idea—he didn't have to try too hard, since I was already pretty much in. "We can shoot locally or you can fly to LA for six weeks at a time. We'll get you a nanny. You can still have time to write. You can have it all!"

It started to dawn on me: TV producers were going to coach me on how to create dramatic tension. I was going to have to wear Spanx for six weeks at a time. And I didn't particularly want my kid to have a nanny. My life would become radically *scheduled*. This was starting to feel very costly.

"I don't think I want to do what it takes for this," I had to eventually confess. "But I thought you said you wanted it all?" said producer guy. "Exposure, influence, to be a big player in this space." Bait . . . baited. That was all true.

"Well, I guess I only want some of it," I sighed. "The some of it that matters most to me."

I drove home from that meeting thinking, *Christ, I think I just walked away from a TV show.* And I felt a momentary wave of panic, because, while I was getting clearer on the life I wanted to live, my creative ambition wasn't decreasing in the least.

I drove home quickly. In ten minutes, my boy would be waiting for me in the schoolyard. Conclusion: I was going to have to find another way to live into the size of my dreams.

MAKE WAY FOR YOUR ART

Art happens in the editing. Writers pour out ideas and images and nuances, but it doesn't become art until it's well-carved and polished. Characters need to be killed off. The sexy headline has to fall by the wayside so that the heart of the story can really take the lead. Every musician has had that one song that they'd love to include on their album, but it was out of place and needed to stay in the vault, at least for that go-round.

The artist understands that destruction is part of expansion and is willing to do what's best for the masterpiece.

Your life is your art. When you make tough choices in favor of your Soul, you're making a masterpiece out of your existence.

To move closer to your Soul, you may leave:

> › your career for your sanity

> › the city for the country

> › law school to tour with your band

> › your band to go to law school

> › security for your freedom

> › your neuroses for your potential

> › common sense for the thrill of it all

Some difficult choices may look like sacrifices at first, until you realize how much you've gained by making them.

ADMIT TO YOUR LIMITATIONS

You have limits.

Budgets.

Sensitivities.

Health stuff.

Emotional wounds.

Kids, parents, families.

Only so many hours in a day.

When you honor your limits—rather than act like they don't exist—you decrease the stress that is sure to creep in when your goals start to test your reality.

ON THE OTHER HAND, SOMETIMES YOU GOTTA RISE ABOVE YOUR SO-CALLED LIMITATIONS

I'm all for mental health days. And gentleness. And I think the world should take the month of December off. And for the love of God, a four-day work-week would revolutionize the collective human spirit and, thusly, health care.

But sometimes, there's another form of self-care: doing whatever it takes.

Just got dumped? Lace up your runners and move your body.

Under the weather? Go in to work anyway, wearing your favorite sweater.

Up to your earrings in deadlines? Go cheer on your friend. Show up at the bake sale. Call your mother.

Crying before show time? Put some tea bags on your eyes. Say a prayer. Enter stage left and . . .

DECIDE

Push. Turn up the volume. Go hard. Go harder.
Reprioritize your aches and pains.
Infuse your sensitivities with courage.
Tell fear to fuck right the fuck off.
Devote yourself to done.

There are Soul-justified reasons to cancel. There are times to just stop.
This isn't one of them. Keep going. Show up. Full on. Full tilt. Full out.
Decide to be one of those people who pull it off.

Do what you say you're going to do.
Don't let us down.
Decide to rise.

Why decide to rise?
Not for the reasons you might think.
In fact, these are the reasons that will make you sick and tired:
Do not rise out of obligation.
Do not rise because of feared consequences.
Do not rise because you think being tough
makes you smarter (it doesn't).

Decide to rise because you want to expand—your being, your life,
your possibilities. Decide to rise because superpowers are meant to
be activated and applied in everyday life.

Decide to rise to explore your place in the universe.

TO RISE

On the other side of deciding to rise is illumination, ecstasy, insight.
And the angel of your strength is there waiting, smiling, applauding,
with a goblet of endorphins for you.
Drink up!

When you transcend circumstances you get special privileges.
You get evidence that you are indeed amazing, and irrefutable proof
that what your heart and mind choose is what matters.

And you get the deep knowing that life wants you to win.

Decide to rise.

Lean in. Listen up. Closely.
It's your Soul speaking, and she says,

Get UP!
I need you.
I want you.
I am you.

Choose me.

Lean in.
Listen up.
Closely.

Decide to rise.

CONFLICTING DESIRES

Let's say you're a mother who works full time and you often feel like you're in the midst of competing wants—even competing core desired feelings. (I'm going to go out on a limb here and declare that you will not find a mother on the planet who doesn't relate to this. In fact, you'd be pressed to find a single human being who can't relate to having some conflicting desires.) Maybe you're the type of mom who'd truly love to have a van full of singing kids, and at the same time, it would be just as natural and fulfilling for you to live alone and not see another person for weeks. Those ideal scenarios seem to conflict, don't they?

Life is full of circumstantial desires that don't easily mesh. How we organize those conflicting wants is the act of designing our lives.

We want to build a business *and* be a competitive athlete. We want to merge our being with a lover *and* strengthen our own identity. We want to be devoted parents *and* have unbounded freedom. Of course we do. You're going to make some tough choices to create the circumstances you want. You're going to go without certain things to have more of other things—and it'll be worth it. You're going to let a few people down—that's okay because you're going to have more love to put where you want to put it. You're going to fumble priorities, but along the way you're going to create your own version of harmony. The havings and doings of your life can find a rhythm, and that rhythm is going to be much easier to find if those havings and doings are anchored to your core desired feelings.

So the next obvious question is, "But what if my core desired feelings seem to compete?" Like, for example, the mom who wants wild fullness and serenity. Or someone who wants to feel stillness and daring, or surrender and determination. If your core desired feelings strongly contrast each other, I have a not-so-philosophical response for you: So what. You are a complex, layered, and multifaceted being. Of course some of your core desired feelings are vastly different and potentially opposing. That doesn't mean you're a split personality or sentenced to a lifetime of option overload. It just means that some of your core desired feelings strongly contrast with each other—because you're that grand.

You'll get your kicks the way you need to. You'll fill your life with children to fuel your desire for bright fullness and, twice a year, you'll head out to a cabin in the woods for a week with nothing but a bag of rice and your journal. You'll do what it takes to feel the way you most want to feel. And when you step back to look at your life it will likely be a mosaic of various types of chaotic and shifting priorities. It may be abstract, it may be fusion, it may be postmodern—but it will be the art of your soul expressing itself in every way possible.

Wanting more for your future is not a betrayal of your present or past.

You are in love with something

That'll tell you who you are

—"Starlovers," Gus Gus

Sometimes dreaming of more than what we've got can feel like it's betraying our current reality. As if wishing for something different means that we're unappreciative of what we have. As if longing for a little less of this, or a brighter shade of that, denigrates what stands in front of us.

While you may feel guilty for doing what it takes to achieve your goals—we'll talk about that in a bit—your actual dreams and guilt should never be in the same room together. They're like the clamps on jumper cables that you never want to cross. If you clamp guilt onto your dream terminal, your desire will get fried into an unrecognizable, unusable mass of electrical confusion.

"I want it . . . but I feel guilty for wanting it." Wires. Crossed. Neither the universe nor your psyche have any idea what to do with that mixed message.

Recognize your preferences and emerging wishes without laying a guilt trip on yourself. Judged desires will make your potentiality very, very cautious. Acknowledged desires whisper to your potential, "It's time to come out into the light."

You're probably going to feel guilty. Maybe you were raised in an environment where desire was considered a negative thing. Or your social circle constantly reinforces the message that you shouldn't dare to bust out. And maybe you frequently feel guilty for wanting what you want—and you *know* that's causing blocks in your life.

So how to vanquish the guilt? How to avoid guilt altogether so you can go get what you want? You can't. You don't. Guilt is part of the deal.

As you craft the life of your dreams, you will experience guilt. It's part of having a conscience; it's the *tension* in "creative tension."

You leave the person who gave you your first big break because it's time to grow. You leave your kid with a babysitter so you can have time to write. You leave behind your mother's idea of success.

You slough off perceived limitations. You go for more. You use brighter colors. You fly higher than they did. You get further than you planned. You let someone down so you can lift up your life purpose.

You're going to feel guilty. Breathe. **The guilt associated with following your heart is a weight you can bear if your desires are strong enough. It's the price of admission to fulfillment.**

MAKE CHANGES WITHOUT CRITICIZING THE PAST— YOUR FUTURE WILL THANK YOU FOR IT

You don't need to burn the dock when you push off your boat. You don't need to diss how you've done things before in order to do things differently now. There's no need to criticize the past in order to validate the future. But we all do it.

We look at how we overworked it, or how we missed the mark, or all the reasons that it, they, you, me, we fell short. We start to shrink the value of the past so that we can justify taking new aim, or giving our notice, or taking the leap that will move us in a new direction. We take a perfectly good essay about our life-learning and accomplishments, and we mark up the margin with red ink notes of all that could have been done differently. Not only does disrespecting how you got to where you are belittle your strengths, but it will also weigh down your transformational process.

How you regard your past influences how your future unfolds. You did what you needed to do at the time with what you had to work with. Thank goodness, praise be, hallelujah! Now let's move on to the part when you have a breakthrough and wake up knowing more. It's not about knowing better, it's about *knowing more.* And now you know where you want to go next.

WHEN TO LET GO OF GOALS THAT NO LONGER SERVE YOU

1. When pursuit of the goal itself becomes a total drag.
A goal that no longer serves you is a goal that doesn't make you feel the way you want to feel while you're going after it. Instead of feeling lit up and enthusiastic, you feel compromised or even a smidge ashamed.

Fatigue is not the same as feeling compromised by or disconnected from your goal. On every journey, at some point fatigue will set in and you'll need to rest or tend to your blisters and your doubts. Nonetheless, you remain committed and proud to stay in the game. It feels exciting to carry on.

If you have to fake excitement about what you're doing, then the original intention is starting to evaporate and it's time to consider pulling the plug.

2. It was somebody else's dream in the first place.
We can inherit ambitions like we inherit eye color and vocal tone. Sometimes inherited dreams are a perfect part of our Soul's unfolding. In divine convenience, we're born into families or cultures that have just the right business or lifestyle for us because it's the exact same one that we're called to live. It feels like a perfect fit.

Other times, though, our dreams run counter to what's prescribed for us by family, culture, or community. That's when we feel like the black sheep whose vision of happiness has no resemblance to where we came from. This scenario gets tragic when the black sheep of the family pretends to really want to be like the white sheep of the family.

A profoundly simple way to get to the truth behind your ambitions is to have your goal in mind and keep asking yourself, *Why do I want what I want?* Ask and answer it a hundred times if you need to, until you hit the *aha!* sweet spot.

**3. It's taking way too long to get there—
and you've been ignoring the stop signs for a long time.**

Yes, there are times to hang in there—come hell or high water—until your final breath. And then there are times when it's obvious to everyone around you that it's just time to move on already.

A story: A couple of friends of mine, Louise and Lance, were best friends. Just friends—they never so much as smooched. They got drunk at concerts together, they slept in the same tent, exchanged great Christmas presents. Lance dated other people. Louise was in love with Lance. Plain as day, all of her friends could see it.

Years went by. New partners and holidays came and went. And it was getting time for Louise to finally lay down her torch. But she decided to make an eleventh-hour pitch to Lance.

This is the crescendo of all romantic comedies, where the protagonist decides to go for it: It's 4 a.m. at one of the best wedding receptions ever. A group of us are smooshed around a corner table, sweaty from dancing, drunk on cheap beer and togetherness. As the DJ starts to pack up, Louise and Lance are the only couple left slow dancing on the floor. We're all staring from the corner, trying to act inconspicuous.

"Oh my, I think . . . yep . . . she's going for it," one of the crew says. "Uh, jeez. This isn't going to turn out s'tho well," slurs another. We lean in, trying to read their lips.

Sure enough, with heart in hand and Cabernet courage, Louise makes her overture. "Do you think we could make a go of it?" Lance is listening. He's one of those good guys who knows when to listen softly. And then, softly, he says: "I think if it were going to happen, well . . . it would have happened by now." Truth bomb. Gently dropped.

If it were going to happen, it would have happened by now.

Even dreams can have an expiry date.

I'm all for fierce faith. But if you're spending an overly long time trying to wish, hammer, hope, push, and ploy things into form, maybe it's time to point your dream in another direction. If a crop isn't growing, the farmer doesn't keep wasting water and fertilizer. He yanks it out, tills the soil, and plants a whole new kind of seed.

Let 'em go. Kill the project. Shut down a division. And take that same longing for love, or creative fulfillment, or phat cash, and face forward.

Hold on to the core desire of the dream—that feeling you want to feel when the dream is realized. But let go of the old target. A new form of satisfaction could be right around the corner.

Just like it was for Louise. She got on with her life. And fell in love with someone who fell crazy in love with her—right away.

4. You're done fighting.
Do you know the story of the man who was hitting himself over the head with a hammer? "Why do you keep hitting yourself with that hammer?" a shocked passerby asked him. "Because," the man replied, "it's going to feel so good when I stop."

Examine the evidence. You keep fighting the same fight. You're losing sleep. You're sick of hearing yourself complain about the same damn things over and over again (yammer, hammer, hammer). You have no fight left in you. This is beautiful! When you have no fight left in you, you can stop fighting to make it work—because, clearly, wrestling with it isn't making things better.

When we stop struggling to make something go the way we want it to, our energy shifts. We surrender to what is, and as hard as it may be, we become willing to face the facts—and we become more present.

The trick is to let a goal go because we're moving on to something more appealing and positive. Like so:

I'm going to stop fighting with this because
I want peace more than anything.

I'm going to stop pushing this, because
I'd rather do something that's way easier.

I'm going to change my mind, because
I've thought of something else that's much more fun to do.

I'm going to change my approach, because
I think I've found a much better way to go about getting what I want.

I'm giving up the fight because I want to be free.

In this way, we move away from a dream not because we're fed up or defeated (even if those feelings led you to this juncture in the first place), but rather because we're moving toward something else we want to feel more—we're choosing ideal. You're not running away or rejecting something. Instead, you've made up your mind that you have some other wonderful things waiting for you and you're going to go pick them up right away.

Godspeed.

RUN TOWARD PLEASURE (NOT AWAY FROM PAIN)

Be suspicious of what you want.

—Rumi

Reputation or self-satisfaction. What the Joneses think or the merit of your own inclinations. The destination or the journey. When it comes to goal pursuit, we're either avoiding pain or seeking pleasure.

PLEASURE SEEKING
When you're focused on the rewards of what you're doing, you're in the driver's seat of your life. Whether the reward is feeling powerful, or the best kitchen that money can buy, or a mental health day off of work, when your intention is fixed on moving forward, toward pleasure, you're taking full responsibility for getting where you want to go.

PAIN AVOIDING

The great fear-based motivators of human nature:

> › What other people think of me: *I better do what makes me look good.*

> › What other people want from me: *I better give them what they expect.*

> › What other people can give to me: *I better play nice to get what I want.*

Your goals are based on avoiding pain when you're focused on getting something so that: you don't lose out; you don't get penalized; you look good to avoid risking humiliation; you don't disappoint people; you can get people to do what you want them to do.

Of course there are positively driven reasons to not want to disappoint people. But fear has a knack of showing up around these kinds of considerations.

The problem with avoiding pain is that your energy is always constricted, so you're more uptight and less trusting. And this kind of stress inhibits your love, your creativity, and your access to your Soul. What's more, when you've been running to avoid the whip, when you do get to your goal it will be bittersweet. As Lily Tomlin put it, "The trouble with the rat race is that even if you win, you're still a rat."

POSITIVE DRIVE

If your choices elicit a full-on *yes!* to any of the following questions, then you're choosing from a place of true creative power. Try these on for size when weighing a particular decision:

> › Is this moving me forward?

> › Do I feel more like myself?

> › Does this clear the way for more good stuff to show up?

> › Will I sleep peacefully tonight?

> › Would my kid [or grandma, or best friend] be proud of me?

Slow down and center yourself to be sure you're being honest with yourself in answering these questions. If you're gripping on to a certain dream, you can easily breeze through something like this and fool yourself. Just a few minutes to tune into yourself, or to work with these questions with a trusted friend, can make all the difference in your clarity.

CHOOSE INSPIRATION OVER MOTIVATION

Like a bird with broken wing
that has traveled through wind for years . . .
I sleep and my heart stays awake.

—George Seferis

Motivation: You run the 5K to lose weight, stay in shape, raise money for cancer. Maybe to prove something. It's on your bucket list. You made a bet. Only five pounds to go.

(These are all fine reasons. Achievement is thrilling.)

Inspiration: The runner's high. My body simply has to run. When I run, I feel closer to life.

Motivation: You write the book, the blog, the brochure to raise your profile so you can sell more stuff, serve more people. You compose 'n' package your thoughts. A thousand words a day until you've crossed the finish line.

(All fine reasons. Getting things finished is a rush.)

Inspiration: I have something to say that needs to be heard. When I write I feel bigger, freer, like life is putting me to good use.

We seem to need motivation to accomplish things. It's part of human nature. Typically there's a lot of measuring that happens in the realm of motivation. Checklists and goalposts and markers and such. There is often a fear of loss involved. We are on duty.

This is all perfectly natural. Motivation is useful—we need it. It's just not the whole story.

Beyond finish lines and a job well done, there is a different call: inspiration.

Inspiration is magnetic and progressive. It's heart-based rather than head-based. Motivation and inspiration both have places in our lives and in our pursuit of desires, but inspiration trumps motivation and it should, in fact, be *leading* the motivation. Inspiration is a completely different force of creativity.

Inspiration's reasoning cannot always be reasoned—you just gotta do it. It's a wellspring of energy. It busts you out of should-dos into the unfenced field of possibility. Inspiration and desire are like king and queen. And motivation is their loyal knight.

What is motivating you? What is inspiring you?

What is pushing you? What is pulling you?

Follow the pull.

It's the first step toward flying.

Subliminal message: Feeling good is the primary intention.

WHAT WE WANT TO DO, HAVE, AND EXPERIENCE

Space to be free, joy to radiate, ease to be me, flow to create, love to begin and begin and begin / Freedom / Peace of mind / Freedom! / It all (And a Buddha bowl from Bridgeport pub in PDX . . . but maybe that's asking for too much) / A bellini sitting out in the sun / Financial freedom. Got love. Got family. / Freedom / A good night's sleep. What? I have a newborn! Someday when I'm well-slept, I want the space (literal and figurative) to write my first novel. / Love / That all souls on this planet may live the life they want to live, and the freedom to choose peace / Calm / Experiences / Freedom I just want now / Love Love Love :-) / love & calm / Peace / To go to Disneyland. With the girls. (I'm sorry . . . that's really what I feel like I want right now: enchantment, friends, and ridiculously expensive churros. Is that bad? I also want world sanity and a cure for cancer. But today, Disneyland would do it.) :) / Profound inner joy and a private jet to get to India faster in a couple of weeks / Nothing I don't have in abundance already / An infinite yes / Peace of mind / Peace at last / To feel more joy! Everything. And nothing. / Adventure and wisdom / To have no secrets from those I care for / Congruency / Joy / Freedom / Love / Quick big answer: to move and live in New Mexico / JOY! / A baby / Self-love / Four thousand euros a month, total freedom, surrounded by spiritual peoples, lots of traffic on my website, esteem, respect, and reconnaissance from others. And to change people lives. That's all for me! ;) / To move in a forward direction / Travel the world, speaking to millions / FREEDOM / Romance / To feel the depth, the breadth . . . the immensity . . . of my own being . . . and know that it is God / Right now in this moment I want a hot steamy ridiculously supportive partnership with my beloved, and whirlwind, simple pleasures, travels, and adventures with my little family! ♥ Thanks for asking! / Peace / To teach creativity / Live life doing what I was meant to do . . . write books and help people and their animals / To believe that I can create my life exactly as I want it . . . right now / To believe it at my core . . . not just conceptually. To believe it like I believe that I can type or walk or chew food . . . so deep that it isn't something I focus on . . . IT JUST IS WHO I AM. / Sustainability. I need all aspects of my life—work, chores, social life, health to just be sustainable. Having chronic illnesses, and therefore limited energy resources, I am working on figuring out a way to make everything easier to maintain/sustain. / Soul mate / Freedom! / Peace / Inner peace, external peace . . . with peace, all other things are not only possible, but simply a given / Energy / Connection—both of the dots (for the vital "oh, I SEE!" moments) and of people / To at all times TRUST that I am creating massive amounts of joy and abundance in my life, and to be grateful for where I am in THIS moment! / In a larger sense, to succeed in my business while satisfying creative needs, motivating colleagues and making the world better at the same time every damn day / Freedom (^_^) / Love all day every day! / Financial freedom, perfect health, my "perfect" partner and overall fun times. Am I only allowed to pick one thing? / Health, joy, love, and sustainability / Freedom from mental chains / These last twenty-nine days at my job to fly by / To be received! / Self-love / To simplify / To fully embrace all that I am now in this moment . . . emphasis on the word "fully" / Accepting all my great quirks . . . standing tall in who I am . . . let it be! / Inner peace / A JOB / I have inner peace and serenity and understanding. / Chakras aligned! / I want to be insanely happy, giggling incessantly in every single moment ♥ / Clarity. Purpose. Contribution. / To really know what it means to be "present" / More time with my horse. To teach yoga at the women's jail. To be done breastfeeding my eleven-month-old twins. / Balance, clarity, and enjoy the simple things with more laughs and not perfection / To be put back on that pedestal / Positive abundant change to live my passion ♥ / To be loved & accepted for who I am / Peace / Clarity, purpose, epiphany, eloquence, and insight in my writing / A life of meaning / My dream job teaching, writing, inspiring . . . / To make a difference / Money to pay for transplant rejection drugs for my husband / Health for me and my family, connection with the Divine, freedom, and peace / Joy / A peaceful life / Security / To feel satisfied and fulfilled / Love and happiness! / The end that will start my new beginning. (Do you hear me, Universe?) ♥ / To be fully me / $$$—I already have love, health, and a majorly blessed life. But, I want to have a business that rocks as much as my husband's seven-figure one does. It feels like a big yummy challenge to manifest my own prosperity separate from the one I enjoy from my relationship. / Love / Find ways to add bike riding to my daily activities, vacations, conversations, and leisure time / To watch my bank balance GROW because I am booking acting jobs in film and TV! / Clarity / Peace / Vibrant health to sustain me through the second half of my life 'cause it looks like I'm starting over from scratch / Enough / Romance / Massive change is necessary. Check out of the NYC rat race. Move to a place in the mountains so mornings can be filled with hiking or skiing, and spend the balance of the day working creatively on things that fill my soul. Evenings by a fireplace with my soul mate husband. / True love with an awesome partner :) / Freedom from the garbage that's weighing me down, holding me back, and generally getting in the way of me living MY life / To make an IMPACT

SINCERE EFFORT, TRUST & FAITH

Trust yourself.
Create the kind of self that you will be happy to live with all your life.

—Golda Meir

FIERCE BUT FLEXIBLE. THE DUALITY OF GOALS WITH SOUL.

Everything matters. Nothing's important.

—Nietzsche

It would seem that there's nothing more dichotomous than having single-minded focus while being detached from the outcome. Holding these two opposing concepts in your mind at once can cause vertigo. But it's this melding of the two, into a kind of **relaxed determination,** that works magic for manifesting.

FIRST, FOCUSED DETERMINATION

When it comes to making your intentions and goals realities, you've got to focus like a *muther*. Like a hungry lioness with cubs to feed, like a pointed laser beam, like a mad scientist who knows that the right formula will happen with enough experimentation and concentration.

I've never seen anyone get anything terrific off the ground without the ability to harness all of their energy and channel it in one direction for an extended period of time. That's why it's called the *power* of focus. Behavioral scientists aren't writing many articles about the power of multitasking. To the contrary, we're mostly hearing about the corrosive effects that split-focus and juggling have on the quality of our creative output.

THREE WAYS TO GET FOCUSED

1. Know the meaningful *why* behind it.
Why are you doing what you're doing? It's not just to make money, to get product out the door, or to please people. Anchor into the truest, most meaningful reason that you've set out to accomplish the particular thing in question. Like, you're doing it to improve living conditions for other people, to

raise consciousness, to spread love, to put your kid through high school, *and* to feel good, of course, which in turn, contributes to everyone's well-being.

2. Become acutely aware of your hunger.
What are you craving that this accomplishment will feed? Your answer to this will directly relate to your core desired feelings. Are you more ready than ever to feel freedom, or to experience your strength, or to transform something ugly into something beautiful? Were you born to do this? Has your time come, gosh darn it?! Are you frustrated and angry in the best kind of way? Are you done taking crap, playing second fiddle, letting someone else dictate your allowable vacation time? Well, are you?!

Deep breath. Regain composure. Good. If you can get riled up about why you're doing what you're doing, then you're not only in touch with the hunger, you're also in touch with your survival instincts. And you're going to need them.

You've got to be hungry. You've got to want it. When I used to do strategy work with entrepreneurs, I noticed that the people who "didn't have to work," or who considered their work to be more of a hobby than a necessity, tended to act more slowly than the ones who needed to make rent or felt like they'd been summoned by the holy spirit to do their work.

Want it so bad you can convincingly act like you *need* it.

3. Get real about what it will take to pull it off.
If ever there was a term wildly open to misinterpretation, it's this: "Be realistic." You have to be extremely particular about how you interpret and apply this term. If you apply "realistic thinking" to your dreams, you may end up crushing them with one silly "realistic" thought form. And we don't want that to happen.

The beginning of the intention-setting process is where realistic thinking *is* actually crucial. First comes the big dream from your heart: "I'm going to create a highly useful something-or-other, because the world needs it!" Awesome! Then, your highly useful brain should kick in and ask, "So what's your intention . . . *really*?" Then you set one: "Launch highly useful something on this specific date." So realism is not to be applied to the size or scope of your intentions and goals, but more to the specificity of their execution. Dream like an eagle, plan like a mouse.

This is precisely where a lot of intentions and goals go sideways. We aim for big stuff—we may even imagine the outcome in extreme detail—but we fail to imagine with the same level of granularity the hard work and sacrifices in other areas of our lives that are sure to come along while heading for our goals. Pulling off your intention or goal might require any number of compromises and sacrifices. Up at the crack of dawn, missing a few birthday parties, opting for a staycation instead of an exotic getaway. Blisters and bruises. Late nights, gluten-free, no TV. A long commute, a shrinking savings account. The patience of Job, the stamina of a steam engine.

Sounds like fun, eh? But actually, when you're moving in the direction of your dreams, the sacrifices can be agreeable—because they don't feel as much like sacrifices. They feel like stepping-stones. Okay, sometimes they feel like monumentally high stepping-stones and you need a ladder to get over them, but still, you're up for it. However, it helps to plan for the foreseeable hardships as much as you can, so that when you meet them, they don't throw you off course too much.

Taking an honest look at the hard part of goal pursuits isn't going to drag down your process or deflate your energy. It's going to help you keep your psyche sharp and your spirit strong.

THEN, EASE UP ON THE EXPECTATIONS

I have willed stuff into being with intense attachment to the outcome. Will-willed-willfulness. And if you had dared to tell me (brave soul, you) in the midst of my willfulness that I should let go of my expectations (gasp!), I would have gone stone cold or laughed it off. Because I thought that expectation was a key ingredient of manifestation. Turns out it can be a major distraction from feeling good—which, in turn, messes with what you're wanting to manifest. Who knew?

Name a major women's lifestyle magazine. Name any one of them. I've probably been to their office, with my best heels on, talking about the meaning of Life and how to be a fire starter, hustling my ideas in hopes of some coverage.

One particular meeting was, in my mind, incredibly high-stakes: "If I land this, it'll change, like, my *grandchildren's* lives." I don't have grandchildren yet—just big dreams. I lost sleep over that pending meeting. I prayed, meditated, worked with my spiritual advisor, rubbed my mala beads, strategized and agonized with my crazy sexy and out-fucking-standing Soul sisters. *Ready as I'll ever be.*

I felt so distracted in the meeting by my underlying agenda, *Gotta gotta make this happen,* that I wasn't my most radiant self. I was cautious and well-behaved. And that kind of shrinking always leaves me with a regretful taste in my mouth, an *if only I had said . . .* kind of haunting.

To my surprise, when I left that meeting, something shifted in me. I had an epiphany on Park Avenue. I thought to myself, *I'm not doing that again. Not like that. I've got nothing to lose, so I'm really showing up next time.* As the adrenaline left my system, I was flooded with a euphoric kind of acceptance and relief.

And then I got it. **Lay down expectations, take up sincerity.** I was still focused on my desires, but I released my grip on the future, and I felt incredibly present.

Intentions? Of course. I love my intentions. Goals? Make them if you need to. Expectations? Ease up on them. Expectations shrink your shine and weigh you down with worry and equations.

Expectation liberation is the new black. Style up.

A PRAYER FOR
RECOVERING EXPECTATION ADDICTS

Lord, Shiva, Yaweh, Saraswati, [insert your own deities here],
hustle my shizzle and deliver me to where it's best.

Yes'm, Jesus, life, cosmic intelligence, Milky Way Magi,
take the wheel.

I know you've got my back.
I know that you know how intensely my heart burns,
how sweet is the honey at the center of my center,
how much I am capable of.
And God knows (that would be you)
how game I am to collaborate with you
to make good stuff happen.

I accept my calling:
To show up and shine.
Unfurled and honest.
Determined to be only that which I am.

I'm here to give my all.

I trust that pure intention counts for plentiful support.
I trust we'll get where I'm going, together.
And I am learning to be where I am.

I'll go make my art now.

I have faith that you've got the rest covered.
The universe will configure around my very best efforts. Willingly.
I can only do what ONLY I can do.

I will do that.

Amen. Om shanti. Shalom.

RESISTANCE

Your resistance is a sign
that your system is reconfiguring itself toward success.

—Todd Herman, thepeakathlete.com

Ever wonder why you feel oh-so-good two days into a new workout regime, only to succumb to lethargy, low self-esteem, and a bagful of Fritos two weeks later? Everything was going so well! You were in it to win it—for real this time!

So, what went wrong?

I have a friend, Todd Herman, who's a sports psychology coach. Like, a top-flight psych coach who helps people win Olympic medals. (*And* he looks like an extra-hot version of Dave Matthews. I digress . . .) Todd has one of the most encouraging and illuminating theories on resistance I've ever come across. And wouldn't you know it—it's backed by hard science.

THE BIOLOGY OF CHANGE

As Todd has described it to me, when you enact a significantly positive lifestyle change (new fitness practice, breaking off a toxic relationship, taking on a new job), your brain temporarily floods your body with feel-good neurotransmitters, such as serotonin and dopamine. It's your brain's way of giving you a high-five.

The happy-drugs start flowing, fueling your good intentions with seemingly boundless energy. Your commitments seem effortless. This is going to be easier than you thought. You've so got this covered.

And then, in a cruel-but-necessary act of nature, the party train grinds to a halt. Your neurotransmitters collapse back to their normal output levels (and thank goodness, because otherwise you'd go crazy, in a literal, clinical sense). And like a rushing river that dries up to a trickle, the rah-rah ferocity dissipates.

You know the progression.

"It goes like this," Todd explains. "Day one, you've got all this energy and drive behind you and you're excited. You go to the gym. You work out. You feel great about it. Day two comes along. You've got the wheels of the train moving forward. Go again. Day three, a little bit of resistance. The tension starts to build up and you go but you're not feeling as great about it. Day four, it's even harder. You don't go on day five. And then . . . no more working out. That's why by the second week of January, the gyms are empty."

At this point, your new, healthy habits are asking your cells to literally alter their shape. And to you, this feels like a major drag.

But in actuality, your cells are loving it! They're vibrating and shifting, doing their own form of yoga. **They're transforming to accommodate your recalibrated levels of positive mood endorphins.** They just need a l-i-t-t-l-e more time to reshape themselves.

This is resistance. And it's cause for celebration. It means that changes are happening.

"Your body is just going through a change, and you're interpreting it as either positive or negative. Really, what you should do is get excited about it. The change that needs to happen in order for your new habits to take form is taking hold. It's taking hold inside your body, " says Todd. "The most difficult part of the journey is the first sixteen days, but then after that, it's a piece of cake. We don't need to think about it anymore. It goes from our conscious mind to our unconscious, or habit mind, where it's happening automatically for us. It's like a wave of positivity that just starts flooding toward you but most people don't see it right away. That happens later."

So, instead of shutting down the new habits when they start to feel unpleasant, we need to shift our attitude toward loving the resistance that arises. Because if we can push through the awkward growth spurt—giving our cells adequate time to catch up with our good intentions—we gain prodigious momentum. Keep on keeping on.

Todd Herman's five techniques for riding out resistance **(with some extra love notes from me):**

1. Breathe.

When you feel resistance building, stop and breathe through it. I encourage my elite-level football clients to take yoga classes for this very reason. Simple breathing techniques will change your game in every area of your life.

2. Grip your power-thought.

Why are you enacting this lifestyle change? What's the end goal? Come up with a power-thought that fully encapsulates why you're doing what you're doing. Hang on to it like a life raft.

Note from me: Your core desired feelings are your power-thoughts!

3. Remind yourself.

"I'm changing." Simply uttering those words—out loud, or inside—will anchor you in reality. It's a trigger. I've got thirteen-year-olds using that trigger. I've got thirty-five-year-old defensemen in the National Hockey League using it, too. It works.

4. Rehearse your performance ahead of time.

It's a powerful way of preparing your mind for what you want to happen. Don't script the outcome—that's too stressful, and there are too many factors outside of your control. Script the process. Script the performance. Script the way you're going to feel.

Note from me: Hello! Did Todd Herman, coach to gold-medal athletes, just say, "Script the way you're going to feel"? Yes, yes he did.

5. Keep drafting.

If your life is a text, and you're the editor, you can make small corrections every day. Editors don't berate themselves when they spot a typo—they don't rip up the whole manuscript and burn it. They just correct it, and move on. Next draft. Self-editing is empowering.

Note from me: Like I said, fierce but flexible.

DO LESS, GET MORE

Desire is this absurdity that holds open the infinity of possibility.

—Wendy Farley, *The Wounding and Healing of Desire*

At some point you're going to think to yourself, "I don't want to work this hard to get what I want." (In work. In love. In life.) It will be epiphanic and very grown-up of you. It will be part of becoming more conscious and more aware that the hard work that we're obsessed with as a culture is overrated. It will be really really liberating.

Take your pick: *I don't want to work so many hours. I don't want to have so many fights about what's not right. I don't want to drive so many miles. I don't want to worry so much, rehearse so much, do so much, hustle so hard.*

This is good. This is very good.

But post-epiphany, we head into very dangerous turf. It's the terrain of unnecessary dream shrinkage.

> Your heart says: *I want to do less.*
> And your head says: *Then you'll get less.*
>
> Your spirit says: *I want to fight less.*
> And your head says: *Then you better settle for less.*
>
> Your body says: *I want more ease.*
> And your head says: *Then prepare to get fat.*
>
> Your intuition says: *I can work less.*
> Your accountant says: *Don't quit that gig yet.*

We think that if we slow down, the dream machine will come to a stop. Or if we stop working so damn hard, we'll have to do without. Or if we stop processing so much, we won't get the deep love we crave.

Simplifying what you put out into the world doesn't mean you have to expect less in return. You can stop with the overtime and overcompensating and still get a raise. You can stop trying to be the most wonderful guy in the room and still attract the right woman. You can ease up on yourself without shrinking your dreams.

The cosmos doesn't measure sweat and hours for reward.

The cosmos deals in the currency of emotion. When we feel good, goodness flows. That means, if kicking back a bit (or a lot) helps you feel happier and more fulfilled, the universe will help you pull it off.

Work simpler and get better results.

Bitch less and things sort themselves out.

Think less and be more creative.

Put in fewer hours and get a greater return.

Hustle less and sell more.

Push less and get further.

TRUST

We *are* desire. It is the essence of the human soul, the secret of
our existence. Absolutely nothing of human greatness is ever
accomplished without it. Not a symphony has been written, a
mountain climbed, an injustice fought, or a love sustained apart from
desire. Desire fuels our search for the life we prize.

—John Elderidge

Before a big gig or a supercharged opportunity, I do a trust ritual with myself.
I started doing it on airplanes to cool my mind down after my strategic wheels
had been turning for a while. Often we're so busy trying to get our endorphins
fired up to *go get 'em!,* we can forget that simply feeling comforted is a very
powerful, and useful, state of being.

Sometimes the fact of the matter is that you don't fully trust that something
will work out in your favor. You have doubts, you're anxious, you have reason
to be cautious—and you're going for it anyway. This is the definition of courage. And it'll be easier for you to courageously go for it if you're anchored to
what's already working in your life.

GUIDELINES FOR CREATING
A "WHAT I TRUST" LIST

1. Focus on the present.
The whole point of this exercise is to access the trust that already lives in
your being. Unwavering. Multidimensionally verifiable. True for you. It's not
about generating new trust, or visualizing outcomes, or affirming your way
into positive thinking. We're concentrating on the now that is already working.

2. Write it out.
It's important that your What I Trust List be written out, not typed up. The
movement, hand to vision, will help your psyche to really take in the comfort.
Imagine that your mind is like a lung, inhaling and exhaling as you account
for all that you know to be true. Ahhhh.

And / or . . .

3. Speak it out.

If you're an audio-learner, speak it out. Leave yourself a voicemail, or record a voice memo on your mobile, or talk to yourself. Kindly.

4. Stream your consciousness.

Just let it pour out—but, again, don't include things on your list that you don't fully have trust in. It's okay if your list is short—brevity is better than bravado. It could be one word if that's what feels true. It could be six pages if that's what's real for you.

I trust my love for my sweetheart. I trust my integrity. I trust how much my mom loves me. I trust that my guides are watching out for me. I trust that he'll be there when I call. I trust that there's always another idea. I trust that I can always get a job. I trust that my car will be there when I get back.

5. Be really obvious if you need to be.

Nothing is too great or too small to put your trust in. Sometimes the most basic and primal things will give you a boost, especially if you're finding it difficult to think of things that you fully trust in.

I trust my next breath will keep coming. I trust the sun will rise tomorrow. I trust Sparky will be wagging his tail when I walk in the door. I trust that the snow will melt.

Trust now.

Trust in the Now.

Consciously access what you know to be positively true. And that sureness will help you strengthen the bridge you're building to what's next.

PRAYER & ATTUNEMENT

I used to pray to sweat blood as a little girl. Dramatic, I know. I was a Catholic schoolgirl, an only child. We rented a small house in a small town, and my parents were young and hip and generally let me do anything I wanted to. The liberal headspace at home, acres of wheat fields to explore alone, and daily Jesus, Mary, 'n' Joseph at school made for the perfect environment for me to become the quietly intense mini holy roller that I was. At one point, I used the nooks of my bookcase to create a home for Barbie, and for the Virgin Mary. A leopard-print chaise *and* a rosary. Heavenly, really.

I prayed. I prayed all the time. I prayed to Saint Anthony, the patron saint of lost things, to help me find my silver bracelet on the railroad tracks. I prayed to Saint Christopher to keep my dad safe on his drive to work. I prayed to Mary to help me see fairies in the woods. I prayed for stigmata to prove that I was on Jesus's team.

In seventh grade I set my sights on becoming a legislative page in the Canadian Parliament. Between the ages of thirteen and fifteen, pages are errand-runners on the Senate floor. In keeping with Commonwealth pomp and circumstance, pages follow meticulous behavioral procedures, wear black uniforms (bonus!), and are privately tutored for the duration of their stay. Hundreds of kids apply for the honor, and fewer than twenty are selected. I had never wanted anything so badly in my tweeny life.

So, I hustled. I wrote entrance essays and got letters of recommendation. And I upped the prayer ante. Father Flynn had told us the story of Christ in the Garden of Gethsemane, and it had made a big impression on me. Jesus had prayed with such fervor and devotion that he had actually sweat blood. *Phenomenal!* I would prove my praying prowess by accomplishing this feat myself.

So, under my *Xanadu* poster and a headboard covered in unicorn stickers, I lay in bed every night for weeks and gave it my all. As if prayer were helium and my skin were a balloon, I tried to float with pure devotion. Within that container of longing, I would plead with the Lord to *Please make me a page* and I would make him proud of me. *Please God, Please God, Please God. Please. Please, please, pleeease.*

Well, the most I could physically manifest was clammy hands. Not one drop of blood. I had failed.

However, in spite of my inability to bleed with benediction, I was awarded a legislative page position that summer. After that, I dialed back my prayer program. Clearly, a good cover letter and pleading with God were enough to get me out of that small town.

The dignity of desire

Dive into the thin air of hope
long for it
like a tree's roots dig
for drink

don't pretend
you don't need it

you need it

but don't expect it to look
like the movie that plays
on the screen
of your skull

your job is not to find it
only to let yourself
be found

to find strength
in begging
for love.

—Samantha Reynolds, bentlily.com

My relationship to prayer has transformed in parallel with my relationship to life. My name for God has changed. My location of God has changed. My capacity to feel God has changed. What I used to call him, I now call Life. What I used to see as rungs on a ladder, I now see as a hologram. What I used to see as out there, I now see is everywhere. *God* is still useful terminology for me. But it's so much vaster than I was led to believe in Catholic school.

As my perception of Godness shifted, or more accurately, as it expanded, I noticed that I was becoming uncomfortable praying. This was really unsettling. Part of the discomfort came from this issue: If I believed God was everywhere, then who was I praying to? If I believed that my true Buddha nature was joy, then what did I even need to pray for? If I believed that everything was progress, then why was I bothering to pray?

This was a conundrum of course, because I didn't want to feel more alone in the universe than I did at the worst of times, and I could certainly do with someone out there pulling cosmic strings for me.

I stopped requesting and started declaring. I went on a request fast. I didn't ask anything directly of Life, and I ceased all prayerful conversation. Around the same time, I also stopped formally meditating. Intentionally. Not like when you don't go to the gym one week and then a month goes by—not that kind of slow halt. I actually declared that I would not sit in lotus or pick up mala beads, or watch my breath for, well, maybe forever.

I'd given up organized religion to feel free, and my meditation practice—which hadn't been that grueling to begin with—had started to feel like just one more thing to do. Meditation had become an assignment for polishing my consciousness, counting my mantras—achieving.

So there I was. Not praying. Not meditating. And I became sincerely concerned that I might drift so far from my Soul that someone skilled in these matters, like a shaman or a Peruvian healer, would have to tow me back to shore. And drift I did . . . but closer to my Soul, actually. Right over to the shore of desire.

Since I could no longer look up to the sky and ask for stuff, and I didn't have meditation to clear my head—but since I still very much wanted to get what I wanted, and to feel generally calm about getting it—I got in the habit of making declarations. *Well, Life, this is what I know for sure: I want this to work out. I want to feel joy. I want to feel better than I do right now. I want to be super creative. Yep, I really really want that.*

Declarations of desire.

I shifted from asking to receive something, and hoping it would be granted, to simply *declaring* my desire in all honesty. I immersed myself in the wanting, not the asking, not the pleading, not the striving, just the very pure wanting. It was the only thing I could verify. It was the only thing I could be sure of.

It became just me, and my desire, and the universe—on common ground. Not a hierarchy, not a waiting game, not a matter of good behavior, or karma, or the law of attraction. And this resolute belief: that Life wants me to have what I truly want—in all ways. And I realized: my *desire* is my prayer.

Desire joins you with God, with Life.

Eventually I started meditating again, but with a clearer relationship to it: for the comfort of oneness, for the gift of sight, to disrupt habits. To be of service with my thoughts and energy. And for **attunement** to my true nature and all that is. For attunement to home—which is where I most desire to be.

May we serve with much fire, much heart,
much desire, and much prayer.

—Ronna Detrick

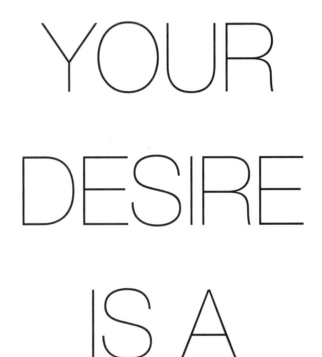

AFFIRMATIONS CAN MESS YOU UP

Affirmations are like screaming that you're okay in order to overcome this whisper that you're not. That's a big contrast to actually uncovering the whisper, realizing that it's a passing memory, and moving closer to all those fears and all those edgy feelings that maybe you're not okay. Well, no big deal. None of us is okay and all of us are fine. It's not just one way. We are walking, talking paradoxes.

—Pema Chödrön, *Start Where You Are*

If you're going to affirm something, affirm the truth.
Then go do something about it.

—Jim Rohn

I came of age in the New Age of the '90s. I had affirmation cards before I had business cards. And I tried to love affirmations, really I did. But affirmations didn't do me any favors. When my mouth was saying, "I am fearless and courageous!" my brain was saying, "I'm scared shitless." So then not only did I still feel scared, I also felt like a fake.

If you say that all is well when all is not well, or that you're skinny when you're feeling fat, or that you're healthy when you're sick—well, to state the obvious, you're lying to yourself. Self-deception creates a cognitive dissonance so that, despite the positive-sounding phrasing, you're creating inner tension and conflict.

Contrived affirmations take you out of the present. Rather than facing what's real, we try to plaster over the difficult truths with happy thoughts. This is false optimism and it's damaging. It undermines our capacity to be with what is and to access our real strength and spiritual maturity. Spiritual maturity includes the capacity to acknowledge our fears while maintaining our confidence and faith.

Affirmations have become a tool for fear management rather than the more productive process of fear analysis, or as Pema Chödrön puts it, "uncovering the whisper . . . moving closer to all those fears." Fear is natural and it deserves respect and compassion—don't insult your fear by smothering it with saccharine affirmations. Be scared. And . . . be brave.

Scientific research proves that positive thinking and affirmative words work. No argument there. Do we need pep talks? Hell yes! Are you the very best person to coach yourself through despair? Hell yes! Do we want to end our suffering and return to limitless bliss and infinite awareness? Yes, yes we do! Do we need to talk ourselves through it? Abso-speakin'-lutely!

So then, speak the truth. Affirm your desire. Declare your intentions. Recall your successes. Your psyche will believe you. Your body will feel you. Your Soul will thank you for the straight-up communication.

You've got an important meeting. You're scared. You really want this to go well.

Look in the mirror and tell the truth: *I'm scared. I really want this to go well. I most desire to feel energized, creative, leadership, and love.* So far, your unconscious trusts you. You're in integrity with yourself. This is actually helpful.

Now if you really want to get your energy up, **state some beliefs:** *I believe in the goodness of humanity. I believe that I've got what it takes. I've got the best intentions and I'm full of creative ideas.*

Keep it up. State some facts, some evidence of your greatness—**recall your successes:** *I nailed this the last time. I won the debate competition. I gave the best wedding toast ever heard. The team raved about my last round of ideas.*

There's more where that came from. You can **give voice to what you're doing that's working in your life right now:** *I see that I am already living this in my relationship with my best friend. I am courageous with my husband. I've been having my most creative ideas ever this week.*

If you want to keep stoking your fire, **pour on the desire:** *I want this job. I really want to feel at ease. I desire for this pain to lift. I desire to be swept away by compassion. I intend to finish first in my league.*

And then really go for it and **state your intention:** *I am going to give this my all.*

All truth. No filler. You didn't bullshit yourself once, nor did you adopt some-one else's projection of your perfect reality.

My friend Bets has a contentious relationship with her sister. It's especially painful because, at one time, they were really close and loving with each other. We were hanging out in my favorite New Age bookstore, after some gluten-free pie and cups of chai, of course, and Bets picked up an ol' affirmations classic. In perfect Mary Poppins dialect she read aloud, "My relationship with my siblings is harmonious. I am supportive and supported." And as she slid the book back on the shelf, she said, "Clearly the broad who wrote this hasn't met my sister."

But being the chai-drinking, New Age bookstore-trolling seeker that she is, Bets knows perfectly well that her outlook has a lot to do with her reality. And so, she told me, she couldn't stomach affirmations but she did do intentions. "I just say to myself, 'I want to be as loving as I can be with my sister.' And that's the truth, and that'll do."

And it does.

Look in the mirror and tell the truth.

State some beliefs.

Recall your successes.

Give voice to what you're doing that's working in your life right now.

Pour on the desire.

State your intention.

DESERVING

You do not have to be good.
You do not have to walk on your knees
for a hundred miles through the desert repenting.
You only have to let the soft animal of your body
love what it loves.

—Mary Oliver

I've been asking around: **What do you think you're entitled to?** And: **What do you know that you deserve?** Here's what some of you have said:

› I'm always curious about this question . . . for me it brings up the distinction between "deserving," which implies reward or merit, and "worthy," which is unconditional.

› I'm not entitled to a damn thing. But I deserve love.

› I don't deserve anything. Everything needs to be earned.

› I'm entitled to be on the planet. I work for the rest.

› I deserve right pay for right work . . . a foot rub and to be fanned and fed grapes . . . no less, no more than any other person.

› I'm entitled to be seen, heard, acknowledged.

› I deserve respect, fun, and money.

› I deserve Love . . . Love . . . Love. We all do.

Deserving and worthiness—these are the notions that get to the pulse of our consciousness and self-esteem.

HEALTHY ENTITLED
VS. GREEDY ENTITLED

So does self-worth translate into entitlement issues? Depends how you look at it. To state the obvious: people with entitlement issues are totally annoying. I had a friend who assumed everything was hers for the having. Let's call her Tina (because that's her real name and this story turns out in her favor). Tina always thought that she was the best person for the job. She'd set her sights on the guy she wanted and go after him without hesitation. She never even considered the possibility that she might be rejected by men, schools, employers, or the bank.

Basically, her modus operandi was, "I want it, so why shouldn't I have it?" And she pushed the envelope even further: "I want it, so why shouldn't I have it . . . *on a silver platter?*" She didn't want to work too terribly hard to get the things she wanted. And at the time, Tina's attitude bugged the shit out of me.

Hold that thought. We'll get back to Tina.

Then there was my stock trader buddy. Let's call him Thurston Howell V (because this story does not turn out so well for "Thurston"). Thurston always thought that he was the man for the job, and that every chick was his to have. He assumed he should have whatever he wanted and that doors should open for him wherever he went—because he was special. And guess what! Thurston's attitude bugged the shit out of a lot of people.

I thought Thurston and Tina were cut out of the same cloth, *entitlement issues* 'n' all, but I started to see big differences between their respective approaches. One of them actually had a *healthy* sense of entitlement. One of them, as it turned out, thought the world owed him something.

When Tina didn't get the job she wanted—because nobody gets everything they want all the time—she was bummed out, but she quickly moved on to the next opportunity. She just figured it wasn't meant to be, and that there was probably something better for her right around the corner.

When Thurston didn't get the gig he wanted, he was shocked and outraged. He'd circle back to find another way in. Even though he still wanted to work for them, he'd put down the people he wanted to work for . . . *Losers*.

When Tina got her heart broken, she took responsibility for her part in creating the relationship scenario and wished her ex-boyfriend well. When Thurston got dumped, it got ugly.

When Tina got acknowledged at an industry banquet for her great work on the job, she thanked her team and talked about how much she loved the vision of the organization. When Thurston got a promotion, he told me, "It's about time, I've been working my ass off for them for a whole *year*." (Poor baby. Twelve whole months!) Tina freely shared her database with anyone who needed a connection. Thurston weighed out the value of introducing people to each other. Would it make him look good?

Tina's definition of the "easy way" was doing the things that inspired her the most—and saying no to the stuff that was a major drag. Thurston's definition of the "easy way" was taking shortcuts that cut other people off.

Healthy **entitlement** believes that everyone is entitled and that there's enough to go around. It's rooted in self-worth and love.

Unhealthy entitlement usually comes from a place of lack and fear. These folks want more than they're willing to give up front. They operate in a fog of emotional and spiritual hunger and conflicting intentions. Often a symptom of deeper wounds from family dysfunction or some other early life trauma, unhealthy entitlement makes people frantic below the surface because they don't trust that they can nourish and nurture themselves.

Vive la différence.

WORTHWHILE

> You can trust the promise of this opening;
> Unfurl yourself into the grace of beginning
> That is at one with your life's desire.
>
> —John O'Donohue

If you don't believe you have the right to be here, there will never be enough space for your true self to show up. If you don't believe that you're worthy of having your desires fulfilled, then you'll always feel more empty than full. No amount of focus or positive thinking is going to help you manifest and sustain your definition of success.

You might fulfill a dream, but if you have a subliminal tape playing in your head that you don't really deserve it, then somehow it'll get washed away as quickly as you manifested it. You'll have a record income one year and then lose a bunch of money on a bad investment. You'll plan the holiday of a lifetime and get sick the first day you land. You'll be a few months into a juicy relationship with a really great person—and you'll sabotage it by doing something completely stupid and entirely preventable.

How can I help you feel worthy? We've come this far together. To this page. This day. I'm struck by this really practical and improbable question: how can I help you feel worthy? If I can get you inspired, I've done something valuable, I hope. But it's really all for naught if you don't feel worthy. You've got to love yourself for yourself. I'm not out to save the world, but since we're here now together, let me give this one a shot.

In real time where I'm at, it's raining on my skylight and I can hear the washing machine spinning. I'm wearing my favorite mocha sweater, leggings, and moccasins. I plan to be here at my keyboard until dark. And as sure as I am that it's raining, that there are moccasins on my feet, and that you're breathing in and out as you read these words, I am sure that you are worthy of having what you want.

You are important.

You are incredible.

You are loved.

Your presence is needed here.

YOU ARE WORTHY OF YOUR DESIRES

A declaration of deserving.
You are worthy of your desires. Really wanting what you want gives you the power to get it. You were born free. (The more you try to earn your freedom, the more trapped you become.) You are worthy of love and respect. Lovable.

You deserve:

> eye contact
> smiles in the morning
> food made with pure intention
> clean drinking water, fresh air
> Hello, Please, Thank you
> time to think about it
> a chance to show them what you're made of
> a second chance
> an education
> health care, including dental
> multiple orgasms
> weekends off
> eight hours of sleep
> play before work
> to change your mind
> to say no
> to say yes
> to have your deepest needs met
> to be seen
> to be loved for who you really are

You deserve all of this—and more—just because you showed up to life.

Maybe you already know this cognitively. Maybe these are the right words at the right time. Maybe you need to read this a hundred times until it feels reasonable. Maybe you need to look in the mirror and tell yourself, *I am worthy,* and feel what happens.

This would be the perfect segue for me to give you a cheese-ball list of *Ten Ways To Love Yourself.* But I have just one suggestion: **Focus on creating your core desired feelings, and as you begin to generate better feelings and experiences, you will feel increasingly worthy of the richness of life.**

When you believe in your birthright to fulfillment, you take the desperation factor out of chasing your dreams. This quells greed—and puts a stop to the winner-loser mentality.

And there's a beautiful twist that happens when you assume your worth: you value other people more. Because when you're operating from a place of wholeness and value, you see value in other people and you reinforce the belief that there's enough to go around for all of us. So in this sense, your self-worth is a service to humanity.

open wide.

give your desires words. out loud words.

tenderly gaze of the eye to eye.

expose your craving any way you must,

under a blanket or backed by a rented band.

reveal your intentions, clean.

stand there, vulnerable, waiting.

describe your dream, in detail.

clarify what you're afraid of and give faith to the opposite.

engage every cell in fiercely wishing:

to be seen. to be graduated. adored. valued. validated. met.

the moment holds it all. give it then and there.

even if it didn't work before, or you're not sure what will come out of you to make for something new.

(you can't be sure.)

blow off the past.

ask for what you want.

unzip the casing of your personality and let that inner layer feel the air. smart warm life.

do it in front of another being.

this is terrifying relief:

to merge

out in front

melting edges

contributing

punctuations of ecstasy

everyday happiness deepening

we know.

pulse open. open. open.

you will get hurt. shattered—guaranteed.

a glance will cut. denial will bruise, rejection will fracture.

you'll cry. clenched. you'll be infuriated. you may choose to walk away—agonized.

leave. quit. swing back. shoot a dart of defence.

you'll regret it—more or less.

if you stay there, closed down 'round your core, then you'll never leave the house feeling like yourself.

you'll pad your soul with stuff destined for landfills.

piles of dislike and complaints will heave between you and bliss.

(bliss is possible. we know.)

itchy. tight. foggy. this happens when the heart is veiled.

nothing will ever be quite right, day after day.

pulse back open.

do it to be it.

lean toward.

worship your precious impulses.

focus to expansion.

this once.

open

up

any

way

you

can.

Book Two:
The Workbook

ESSENTIAL. THE HEART OF IT ALL.
THIS IS WHERE YOU SIMPLY MUST GO.

THE DESIRE MAP
AT A GLANCE

LIFE AREAS

LIVELIHOOD & LIFESTYLE

career. money. work. home. space.
style. possessions. fashion. travel.
gifts. sustainability. resources.

BODY & WELLNESS

healing. fitness. food. rest
& relaxation. mental health.
sensuality. movement.

CREATIVITY & LEARNING

artistic and self-expression.
interests. education. hobbies.

RELATIONSHIPS & SOCIETY

romance. friendship. family.
collaboration. community. causes.

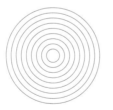

ESSENCE & SPIRITUALITY

soul. inner self. truth. intuition.
faith. practices.

Key questions you'll explore:

> In every area of my life, **what am I grateful for? What's not working?**

> **What are my core desired feelings?**

> To generate my core desired feelings, **what do I want to do, experience, or have?**

> What **three or four intentions and goals** will I focus on **this year?**

> What will I do **this week to generate my core desired feelings** and fulfill my intentions and goals for **this month?**

OPTIMIZING

MAKE IT SACRED

Let this process be important and sacred for you—because it is. You're a grown-up, so do this in whatever ways feel inspiring to you. You know how you learn best and what you need to hear yourself think. Crank some rock or rock opera if that's what alters your state. Light a honey beeswax candle (because those cheap petroleum-based candles are bad for your lungs). Find a park bench, get a sitter, say a prayer. Do what you need to do to create a container that will allow you to unfold your truth.

And if life is nuts right now for you, forget so-called sacred containers and making Zen space. Do this on the subway, sneak it in between client meetings, do it in the car while you're waiting for the kids to get out of school. **The sacred shows up whenever and wherever you call on it.**

CREATE SPACE

You may be able to do the entire process in one sitting—a quiet afternoon when your head is clear, a late night when you feel most alive. This is a very elastic, personal process. It takes some people a few hours; it takes other people two weeks. You may set out to do it all at once and wind up needing a break, or it could go way faster than you imagine.

But the average time for most people to travel through *The Desire Map* is a few days if they're intent on it. **You'll likely want to pause between some of**

the exercises. Specifically, you'll probably want to take a break once you've identified your core desired feelings and before you move to the next stage of setting goals according to those feelings. You may want to look up definitions of words and let them roll around in your psyche while you're making dinner, or during a good night's sleep.

This is deep work presented in a streamlined way. I like to expedite learning, but not skate over what's most meaningful. And very often, the truth of things needs some time to surface. So stay focused and intent, but know that there's no reason to rush or, on the other hand, draw out the process. Go at your own pace.

Some people prefer to do this with a partner or a group. They find that the interactivity of shared reflection and being seen and heard by another helps make things clearer and more vibrant. For others, this is a solo expedition and they wouldn't have it any other way.

BEND THINGS TO FIT YOU

There are five life areas:

LIVELIHOOD & LIFESTYLE

BODY & WELLNESS

CREATIVITY & LEARNING

RELATIONSHIPS & SOCIETY

ESSENCE & SPIRITUALITY

There are a thousand and one ways to slice life and, to some degree, any division of it into categories is, admittedly, a bit forced. It's all connected and of a piece, really. However, these categories are meant to help you focus. But if these themes overlap for you and you want to rename them so they better suit your lifestyle and interests, please go right ahead. The boundaries are fluid here.

We're going to start with some yoga for your inner self, followed by some gratitude and constructive critiquing, and then we're heading full-tilt toward your desires.

SOUL LIMBER

Take a journey into the things which you are carrying, the known—
not into the unknown—into what you already know:
your pleasures, your delights, your despairs, your sorrows.
Take a journey into that, that is all you have.

—Jiddu Krishnamurti

This is a warm-up. We're circling your desires before we dive straight into them.

The Q&A on the following pages is meant to loosen some of the calcification from your intellect and get you closer to your heart. We need to get you out of your head—because that's not where your truth springs from. Your mind helps you act on your feelings. It's your strategist and your activator. But your core desired feelings come from the center of your heart.

Some of these questions may strike you as abstract or esoteric. They get increasingly poetic as you go. You may not be familiar with a term, or you may be suspicious about a question's aims. That's just fine. This is an open-ended inquiry designed to get you to leap to your own conclusions and be impulsive. I'm nudging you to think deeply and quickly.

You can go with the first answer that comes to mind, change your answers, or jump all over the pages. You can give one-word answers or cram in as many thoughts as you can fit into the space.

Further into the desire-mapping process—especially when we get to identify-ing your core desired feelings—I'll be asking you to really think things through. So you may want to pace yourself now, plan to do this in multiple sittings, or just prepare to burn some serious Soul fuel—it's a renewable resource. So I say throw caution to the wind and pour yourself into every step.

Park your brain, engage your spirit.

Stream your consciousness.

There's no right or wrong, just here and now.

RAPID-FIRE STARTING

I crave

love   freedom
coffee   travel
chocolate
to be hungry
to be wanted
to be desire
be taken seriously

Other than time or money, what I want more of is

patience   home
happiness
grattude
acceptance (myself + others)
experiences
love

I need to give myself more permission to be

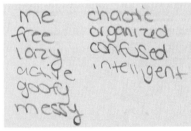

me   chaotic
free   organized
lazy   confused
active   intelligent
goofy
messy

What's different about me is that

Im quirky   I want happiness over $
weird
emotional/sappy
I love too much + too deeply
I hurt often
I protect those I love

What do I do most naturally?

care
feel
help others
communicate w my freinds
share

What do I do even though I don't want to?

show up   compromise
talk on the phone
pay bills
wake up early
go to bed
say no
say yes

Light and heavy: This brings me alive, enlivens me, reminds me of who I am

children
reading
crafting
being around my family
being at home
travelling
making bad choices shows me who I am

Light and heavy: This depresses my spirit, weighs me down, down, down

melancholy
feeling fat
being rejected/bailed on
comparing my image of my life
social media comparisons

PSYCH SURFING

The best advice I've ever given

you have to do what you want and whats going to make you happy

The best advice I've ever received—and I'm glad I took it

do you want to be comfortable or happy?
the universe has your back

The best advice I've received and didn't follow—and I'm glad I ignored it

you are too smart to throw that away and not go to grad school

I get through tough times because

Im strong. I can handle it. I always bounce back.

When in doubt

write about it. cry. scream. sing. dance vent about it. call mom.

My joy comes from

being around kids and making them smile. cuddling with Jon. being around my loved ones

I value

friendship   humour
Honesty*   sillyness
loyalty   selflessness
love
truthfulness

I believe in

love
my mothers love for me + my sister
myself
my dreams

I'm dead set against

being vindictive, manipulative, greedy, perceived as total bitch
- pushing ppl over to get own way

What I know to be true

my next breath will come
the sun will shine again
the summer is coming
my love for Amanda
my love for my family

SENSATIONS OF POSITIVITY

The color of joy

yellow

The sound of joy

babies/kids laughing
uncontrollabley

The scent of joy

lavender
smell of rain +
fresh washed sheets on the line

Love smells like

Vanilla   fresh linen
Cinnamin
cloves

In my body, appreciation feels like

I know I'm happy when

> i catch myself smiling
> singing out loud to my music
> Im dancing aromatice house

If delight were an animal, it would be

> a dancing, jumping fox

Ecstasy lives

> in my heart and brain
> → ecstasy takes over all my senses live
> to glve in

Pleasure feels

> like my body tingling all over
> being sensitive to every physical thing

When I whisper the word bliss

> it slows my breathing
> makes me listen
> opens up my heart

RELATING TO LIFE

I was on Kauai, reading Eckhart Tolle's *A New Earth* on the beach, and this question of his became my walking, rambling meditation:

"What is your relationship to life?"

Daunting. Galvanizing. Spectacular.

It opened the floodgates of inquiry for me. I spiraled backward to look at my relationship to my man, my child, my families of blood and Soul, my portals of connectivity and communion. This led me to a question of my own that turned out to be just as crucial: how do I relate to people? And it occurred to me that **how we relate to people is how we relate to *Life.***

I saw a pattern of truth emerge for myself, a through-line in all of my inter-actions with everyone. Whether it is my best friend or the dude who hands me my rooibos tea at the café, there is a consistent energy and attitude that I bring.

The rhythm of it goes like this: I send out a honey-golden love: "I love you— we're in this together." I make an energetic declaration. It's pure and it's inno-cent and it's graciously global.

Then I start calculating and surmising. "I get you. I see you." And I can't tell if it's intelligence or my heart starting to contract with fear, but somehow a "Don't fuck with me" vibe slips in there. And I end up at this: "You do your thing and I'll do mine."

When I looked at my relationship to people (and I count my dog as a person) it became clear that I am a planet of love with a hair-trigger drawbridge that can close without much warning. I can be—and this was somewhat heart-breaking to realize—somewhat reserved with my love.

And thus, my relationship to Life: Big Love. True Smile. Tricky Lock. My work is in progress.

RELATING TO PEOPLE = RELATING TO LIFE

With people, I'm

pretty open   reserved
energetic
positive
shy/quiet

I feel vulnerable when

I don't know anyone
I have no common ground w people*
Im critiqued
people whisper around me

What feels ever-present and steady within me is

- my ability w children, never
  doubt I'm good w kids,
  I know I'm a nurturing person
- that I have a lot to offer the world

When I'm feeling free and strong I tend to

read a lot   talk to amanda
craft
be outside
seek other like minded souls
smile a lot

I keep in reserve, locked up, and hidden away

my insecurities
the parts of me that are melancholic/depressed
that I'm afraid of losing it all

I'm frightened

to lose my family
to wake up and not know how my life turned out
as it did
to not have my children

I'm greedy with

my mans time/attention
matches frondships
wanting to be the child expert

I'm proud of

my ability to live on my own and be ok
to come back from my breakup with a new
sense of strength + sense of love for myself
my ability to get what I want

When I engage with people my most frequent motive is

to get to know them
-be part of their wonderful lives

I'm trying to impress

my mother
family
friends
myself

In crisis

I breakdown   talk to my mom
cry   listen to daughter
fight
~ignore people

When I'm generous, I

give everything I have
go out of my way
feel helpful

I stop being generous when

im unappreciated
Im mentally exhausted
I get nothing in return ever

What moves and touches me deeply

true human emotion
when a child tells me they love me / like me
someone does something for me bc they can
genuine sincerity

My most regular waking thought

I want more

My favorite feeling

so happy I could / being on the dancefloor
burst / and feeling complete
bliss

GRATITUDE & WHAT'S NOT WORKING

I will not hide my tastes or aversions.
I will so trust that what is deep is holy.

—Ralph Waldo Emerson

GRATITUDE PUTS EVERYTHING INTO PERSPECTIVE

We're going to explore what you're grateful for in your life so that you can a) get some positive emotions swirling and bring your vibration up, and b) get clearer about where you want to focus your creative energy.

Make your gratitude lists as long as you want! Yep, the longer the better.

Specificity increases the sensation of appreciation. In the book *The Happiness Advantage,* Shawn Achor suggests that one of the reasons why gratitude lists are sometimes less effective than they could be is because we often list the same things over and over again and they're sort of general, like "my family" or, "my house." But if we get more specific, like, "I'm grateful my sister and I fall into fits of giggles every time we get together," or "I'm grateful my house is the perfect temperature today," it creates a deeper sensation of gratitude in us than just general listing does.

Next to each thing that you say that you're grateful for, you'll be asked to complete this statement: "I'm grateful for this because . . . " The reason I'm asking you to qualify why you're appreciative is because, again, it helps to expand your awareness of gratitude and illuminate positive feelings—some of which you may later discover are your core desired feelings. Again, this is your process, so feel free to skip this layer if it starts to feel like a grind to you.

WE NEED TO GET REAL ABOUT WHAT'S NOT WORKING, SO THAT WE CAN CHANGE IT.

I think it's healthy to get real about the negatives in your life so you can make a plan to transform them, or at least to consciously ignore them and, instead, focus more of your attention on the positives (in which case, some of your so-called problems often tend to disappear).

Next to each thing that you say isn't working, you'll be asked to complete this statement: "Why this is causing me dissatisfaction . . ." Your answers may surprise you.

That said, we don't want to turn this into a bitch fest. So I suggest you keep this part of the conversation brief. We really do want to make a practice of accentuating the positive in our lives, so consider the "What's not working" sections just pit stops along your appreciation highway. Keep your time there to a minimum, focus on the critical issues, and get back to the upside.

YOUR
CORE
DESIRED
FEELINGS

This is it.

Here we go.

CLARIFYING YOUR CORE DESIRED FEELINGS. THIS IS THE WHOLE, IMPORTANT, BEAUTIFUL REASON WE'RE HERE.

This is where you feel out the shape of your heart. It's time to put your ear to your psyche and listen to the hum of your longings.

Here's what you're going to do: You're going to riff on how you want to feel in the key areas of your life, and then you're going to narrow down those feelings into some core desired feelings. Shazam. I'm making it all sound very easy. And it can be. But this does require a focused heart and an open mind.

START WHERE IT FEELS EASY

You can start desire mapping in any number of ways. You can go through each life area (wellness, relationships, and so on) one at a time and in sequence, or you can drop into whatever sections feel the easiest, richest, or most fun to you first.

This could be really easy. You don't need to tackle this material. Do yoga with it. Let me plant the seed that this can be an incredibly fluid and energizing process if you just intend for it to be. You can make a wish right now, or an out loud declaration: "I'm going deep with grace, and I'm coming out with plenty of liberating illumination."

This could make you sweat. Toil and fret if you need to. Get frustrated. Grind out your anxieties. Rub words down to their nub. Most worthwhile clarity involves some degree of friction.

You might cry—with relief, with a sense of sadness about being out of your Soul zone, with the beauty of feeling into your heart more than ever. You might sigh and let out those breathy gasps of *aha* realizations, the pleasure of recognition that you know what you want . . . and you're committing to going for it.

TOOLS YOU MIGHT USE

You may want a dictionary and/or thesaurus to refer to. I'm a fan of dictionary. com, and there are also free thesaurus and dictionary smartphone apps. You might want to have a few colored pens for writing and highlighting.

I also think that a hot pot of herbal tea and some dark chocolate are essential—or whatever your cherished libations are. Silence—ahhh. Or music!

GIVE WORDS THEIR POWER

Words. Feelings. Feeling words. Words that make you feel. Feelings that can be captured in words. We're going to honor the immense power of singular words. Every word is its own universe. Words have never mattered more than they do here.

This exploration is about the vibration of words. You want to home in on the feeling words that *really* resonate with you. They click. They inspire you. They feel juuust right.

KNOW THAT YOU KNOW

This isn't an exam. There's no test. This is a laboratory for your consciousness and a playground for your aspirations. So much of our truth is right under the surface; it only takes a light scratch and a clear wish to evoke it. You know the answer.

If you feel like you might have trouble accessing how you want to feel, then you can warm up by thinking about how you don't want to feel, and then aim for the opposite of that with your desired feelings.

Recall a few times when you DIDN'T feel the way that you wanted to.
You got your hopes up. You had expectations, cravings, ideals—all dashed.
You were surprised by how you felt. Turned off. Embarrassed. Sad. Empty.
Enraged. Anxious. Disappointed. You just did not feel how you would have
liked to in the particular situation.

feelings.
emotions.
sensations.
states of being.
sensing.
mood.
awareness.

Recall some times when you felt the way that you were hoping you'd feel.
Yes! A day you'd been dreaming of that turned out ideally. A rush of gratitude when it all worked out. Sweet relief when you got where you were going. A flood of love when you made the connection. Unencumbered positivity.

feelings.
emotions.
sensations.
states of being.
sensing.
mood.
awareness.

HOW DO YOU WANT TO FEEL IN EACH OF THESE AREAS OF YOUR LIFE? RIFF . . .

Stream of consciousness is the way to go here. Ramble, jam, repeat yourself. Don't be concerned with duplicating words in different areas.

A desired feeling doesn't have to be summed up in just one single word. For example, "turned on" works. So does "at one with nature," or, "passionately engaged."

Anything goes. Get abstract or specific. Do you want to feel *spicy* or *red* or *electric*? Do you want to feel ten different ways of confident? Then just write it down. Close your eyes and tune in. Let your wanted feelings flow freely. Do not censor yourself. Go deep, yet keep it light.

Let it flow, but you don't have to push yourself to come up with a huge number of words for the sake of variety. If you have only a few words in each section, then you might already be close to the heart of your matter.

LIVELIHOOD & LIFESTYLE

career. money. work. home. style.
space. possessions. fashion. travel.
gifts. sustainability. resources.

Within my LIVELIHOOD & LIFESTYLE, I want to feel . . .

BODY & WELLNESS

healing. fitness. food. rest & relaxation.
mental health. sensuality. movement.

Within my BODY & WELLNESS, I want to feel . . .

CREATIVITY & LEARNING

artistic and self-expression.
interests. education. hobbies.

Within my CREATIVITY & LEARNING, I want to feel . . .

RELATIONSHIPS & SOCIETY

romance. friendship. family.
collaboration. community. causes.

Within my RELATIONSHIPS & SOCIETY, I want to feel . . .

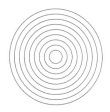

ESSENCE & SPIRITUALITY

soul. inner self. truth. intuition.
faith. practices.

Within my ESSENCE & SPIRITUALITY, I want to feel . . .

STEP 2
GET INSIDE THE WORDS. LOOK UP THE DEFINITIONS OF THE WORDS THAT YOU WROTE DOWN.

It's dictionary and thesaurus time. Every word is its own world. Dig deeper. When you read the actual definitions, do the words take on a new, or more powerful, meaning to you? Do they feel more masculine or feminine? What nuances are in the words that you relate to? Do the origins of certain words inspire or repel you? Do you have a positive or negative history with that word?

Grow. Add new words if you want to. Do you see new feelings in the thesaurus or definitions in the dictionary that you gravitate toward? Write those down as well.

Official word definitions don't always match up with contemporary understanding or our personal vibe. You may find that some words that you really love have sort of old-school moralistic definitions that turn you off to the words. Ultimately, you have to define each word for yourself; it only needs to fit into your psyche, not Webster's history. You can either let the dictionary definition play into your word choices and impressions of the words, or choose to go with your own intuitive connotations and even revise the dictionary definitions based on your own experiences.

Again, there is no right way or wrong way to approach this. If you're feeling like you're swimming in definitions, then back away from the dictionary and go back to what feels easy. If you're feeling like your words aren't spiritual enough or sophisticated enough by someone else's standards, then give yourself permission to keep it simple, because simplicity can be very freeing.

STEP 3

MAKE YOUR FIRST PICKS. GO BACK TO YOUR RAMBLE OF WORDS AND CIRCLE THE ONES THAT RESONATE WITH YOU THE MOST.

Try to select about ten words or fewer. You can always put a word back in the mix if you pass it over in this first round. Don't stress about it—this is supposed to feel fun and exciting.

Trust yourself here. The truth wants to surface and you are creating space for it to rise up.

Here are some different approaches and questions to help you explore your relationship to various words:

Ask yourself which words make you feel *positive, uplifted, expanded.*

Which words feel like home? Which make you feel inspired, grounded, peaceful, energized, or supported? **Circle them.**

Approach each feeling word from every possible angle.

Ask these questions of each word:

> › What does it **feel** like to be [insert word]?

> › What does it **look** like to be [insert word]?

> › What does it **sound** like to be [insert word]?

> › If I were [insert word], **what would my life be like?**

And this abstract question might unlock some clarity for you:

> › **What's** [insert word] *really* **about for me?**

For example, maybe "confidence" is really about feeling empowered, or elegant, or it's about respect. Maybe "success" is really about freedom, or love, or being collaborative. Maybe "beautiful" is really about connection or radiance.

Be especially vigilant in looking beneath big, sweeping concepts and words such as "successful" or "confident." (I can tell you from having this feelings conversation with over a thousand people, just about everybody and their brother wants to feel successful or confident in some way.) These broad types of words might not give you the potency of motivation you're looking for.

Which words have the same or very similar meanings? To make your binary choices, it can be helpful to look up the definitions of the words—or just follow your heart. Either way, you can't go astray.

Do you have strong emotions around some words? Some words might make you want to laugh or cry. Pay extra close attention to the words that stir your emotions—those feelings are trying to show you something.

Do you have a sense of pressure or proving yourself around a certain word? Let me give you an example of this kind of experience. While desire mapping, Jules kept coming up with the phrase, "fully realized." She started wondering, what if she did indeed create the feeling of "fully realized" in her life? Might that mean that she was done with her creative growth? What's left in your life after you're fully realized? Not much room to grow. But she was still attracted to it and left it on her short list of word choices anyway. This is good. She hung out with the wording a little longer to see what was there for her.

Further on in the process, when she asked herself what the phrase "fully realized" *was really about,* she had a eureka moment. "I was shocked to discover that my desire to feel fully realized was basically about wanting to prove something. My anxiety around that phrase was brought to clarity and I was able to cross it off my list with confidence."

It may be a process for you of *grapple and examine, grapple and examine.* That's great, because that will lead to clarity. If you're confused about a word or having a hang-up about it but still feel compelled to keep it on your list for some reason, trust that the process will take you where you need to go with that word and your relationship to it.

STEP 4
PATTERN RECOGNITION.
PREPARING TO HOME IN.

You're going to notice some of the same feelings and words repeating themselves throughout your answers. This is good because, in both theory and practice, we tend to reach for the same feeling states across all areas of our lives. If we want to feel "vital," we want it in our relationships and in our careers. We want to feel "creative" with our business and with our style. We might want "connection" as much with our Creator as we do with our own bodies.

Focusing on core feelings is a critical part of this practice. Core desires equal unlimited power. If you have a lot of desired feelings on your list, it makes it more difficult to prioritize. Choose the words that are so precise that they feel electric.

We need to zone in on the *core* desired feelings that you want. Ideally, you want to choose three to five core desired feelings. We're not going for a vast array of emotions; rather, we want a compact foundation of feelings. Think of it this way: we want the North, South, East, and West of your compass, not every street that you could turn down.

Now you want to find the redundancies and overlaps between various words so that you can knock some words off your list and zero in on the most empowering selections for yourself.

A gentle cautionary note:
A root theory in this whole methodology is that we're not relying on the external world to make us feel a certain way, nor are we blaming circumstances for our emotions. We're taking charge of our own fulfillment.

I certainly want you to find terms that are not just inspiring, but comforting and soothing. But let me point out something about the subtle but powerful way in which words can orient our energy. They can steer us to look outward, or they can anchor us in looking inward, so we're either consciously looking to our inner power or unconsciously looking to the outside world for what we want.

Say this phrase:
"I want to feel loved."

Now say this:

"I want to feel love."

Do those sentences feel different to say? They do to me. *Love* as a noun feels more centered and open, more empowering. *Loved* as a state makes me feel like I'm waiting for someone to love me. And that definitely doesn't feel as powerful.

Here's my gentle point: be really mindful about using terms for feeling states that come from the outside world, as they can set you up to expect that Life (or your partner or your job) is going to make you feel that way.

Here are some examples of feeling states that might depend on external validation: *respected, cherished, admired, honored, seen, heard, adored, treasured, loved.* These feeling words seem to rely on outside sources to make you feel them.

On the other hand, here's another subtle distinction that I want to bring up. Some of us have a tendency to overgive. This tends to be more common for women. We're always in the mode of loving or nurturing, organizing, creating, beautifying, motivating.

If overdoing, overperforming, or overgiving is your issue, then you need to be aware of words that keep you in do-mode. Basically, be mindful of verbs. For example:

Say this phrase:
"I want to feel loving."

Now say this:
"I want to feel love."

Loving as a verb is something you have to do. Yes, being loving is one of the most delicious and nutritious ambitions a human can have. And for some of us, "loving" as a core desired feeling would be the perfect fit. But if you choose a doing word because you think you need to improve, or catch up, or prove yourself, then you're shortchanging yourself.

Remember: you know the answer. This is your domain, your spirit. And this is deeply personal work. As Carl Jung put it, "Only the dreamer knows the dream." The meaning of each word or phrase is for you to own and interpret. It does not have to fit a formula. It doesn't have to be workable or realistic for anyone else — not even your best friend or therapist. Dream your dream. Feel your feelings. Aim.

STEP 5

MAKE YOUR FINAL PICKS: CHOOSE YOUR THREE TO FIVE CORE DESIRED FEELINGS—AND SHINE, BABY, SHINE!

This is the moment! I'm thinking of you right now, sending light and whispering into your ear: The core . . . desired . . . feelings. Oh yeah.

If you want to keep more than five feelings, go right ahead. If seven is your lucky number, then go ahead, choose seven words for luck. Focus might help you get better results, but doing it in the way that works for you is what's most important.

Write your core desired feelings on the following page.

One more note about the process: I'll be asking you to write down your core desired feelings in numerous sections of the workbook—repeatedly. You'll be writing them out many times. There's a practical reason for this: to make the workbook your own reference. But there's also a psychological reason for it: the repetition of rewriting your core desired feelings helps you to anchor them into your heart and mind. This is a process of rooting and integration.

MY CORE DESIRED FEELINGS

BRAVISSIMO!

You've homed in on your core desired feelings. Brilliant. Some people go their entire lives on an autopilot of do-get-do-get, but you've just cracked the code to wide-awake living. In the next chapter, we're going to **weave your inner awareness into your action plans.**

A few thoughts for now:

LET IT STEW

Don't tattoo your core desired feelings anywhere —yet. **Move on to the next phase of desire mapping, but know that this can be a trial run.** You can feel out your words for a few weeks and go back and tweak them for the exact fit. This is an art, not a science. Feelings are fluid and this practice should be as well.

BE OPEN TO CHANGE

Will your core desired feelings change over time? Maybe. I worked with the same feelings for a few years, then refined them more and really landed on the right ones (I'll tell you more about that in a few pages). I suspect some people might want to choose new core feelings every year for the sake of experimentation. On the other hand, what you nail down this week may serve you for the rest of your life. The important thing is to stay curious and alive with your core desired feelings. If they don't keep their glow, you can't use them as a guidance system.

COMPARE NOTES, BUT DON'T COMPARE YOURSELF

Sharing your discoveries with a friend is a great thing to do. Just be sure to avoid the trap of hearing someone else's desires and then changing your own because you've now decided they are less awesome, cool, or noble than the other person's.

TRY THEM ON FOR SIZE

Now might be a good time to write your core desired feelings in your planner, or on some sticky notes. Text them to yourself. Post them on your fridge and your bathroom mirror; keep them by your bed. You want to see them throughout the day and start relating to them.

NOW: REST

Take a breath. Take a hot bath. Walk around the block. Do some kitchen disco.

Have a good cry, call a friend, make an orgasm happen, stretch.

You've just done some good Soul-searching and surfacing. Before you jump into the next phase of writing out your core desired feelings and matching them up with visions and to-dos, it's a good idea to let yourself pause and integrate.

Be gentle with yourself. Your truth is rooting more deeply into your cells. Let your ideas percolate and even infiltrate your thinking and the way you are viewing yourself and your actions and your life.

Take a break—for an hour or two or for a couple of days. I'll be here when you get back.

And please, do come back. Don't stay away for too long—we're now in the valley where ideas meet actions, and dreams are made manifest. The view is stunning from here: miles of desires.

INTERMISSION

THE EVOLUTION & WORDPLAY OF MY OWN CORE DESIRED FEELINGS

Each of us will traverse our desired feelings in different ways and to varying depths. Since desire mapping is a practice that I created for my own life and want to share with other people, I've been motivated to refine this process to its most effective form. I've worked it over and over again until it worked me. Fortunately, I'm a slightly neurotic, overly analytical, spiritual idealist. And I'm just self-centered and poetic enough to care about the nuances of words and how they affect my psyche. This is good news for all of us.

Here's my personal journey with my own core desired feelings. Welcome to my headspace. Please walk softly.

TRADING UP MY THOUGHT FORMS

For a while, I forgot about this process. It was just a simple little thing I did on New Year's Eve, and I thought it was still better for me to do some traditional goal setting. I let the sticky note of my four preferred feelings get buried in my day planner. I planned my days according to the accomplishments that seemed shiniest to accomplish. I went about my business. In that less conscious mode, I did some things that I didn't really love doing. I took on some projects that didn't light me up. I bought shit that I didn't need.

And I got slightly worn down—like we do when we press forward too long without a Soul tune-up. It wasn't a breakdown kind of fatigue that I was feeling, just a slight but ever-present strenuousness to my life. It wasn't as smooth as I longed for it to be.

I knew in my heart that I was definitely heading in the right direction. My career and creativity were great sources of joy, my friendships were deeply loving, my house felt like a sacred, stylish hive. But even though I knew I was in the fast lane, on course, I felt like I was driving an old station wagon with a faulty clutch, instead of a shiny new Porsche. I was in the right lane, but grinding my gears. On one particularly hard-grinding day, I looked at my overstuffed email inbox while drinking cold tea at half past midnight, and I said aloud to my computer screen, "This is *not* how I want to feel." I was spending too much time reacting to the demands of my business instead of doing what I loved to do most: making new stuff. I was feeling like a sales-man under quota, too disconnected from my light—not particularly super sexy. I pulled out my calendar, and in the top margin of "This Week," I wrote:

> Divinely feminine.
> Connected.
> Innovative.
> Affluent.

I felt better already.

I focused on those same core desired feelings for about four years. They didn't change at all—they felt juuust right. As desired feelings go, divinely feminine, connected, innovative, and affluent proved to be great guides for manifesting. They resonated with my spirit and helped me make some of the best choices I've made in my life—small choices and monumental choices. Daily choices and once-in-a-lifetime choices.

RECALIBRATING THE COMPASS

After a few years, I felt compelled to revisit my core desired feelings to do some psychic spring-cleaning. I looked at each word to see if I was still resonating with it.

> Was this desired feeling still **pulling me forward** in my life?
> Was it what I was **currently craving**?
> Was the word itself as **precise and luminous** a symbol as possible?
> Was I truly **embodying** these feelings?

In asking these questions, I started to see my relationship to the actual words in a clearer light. When I said to myself, "I want to feel affluent," or "I want to feel divinely feminine," I often felt as if I was pointing to something outside of myself, like the feeling would be delivered *to* me, not necessarily *from within* me. That was not quite right. The words were off a smidge.

A guru once told me that when we say, "I love you," we really should be saying, "I am love." Translation: OWN IT. We are the source. This inspired me to try on my core desired feelings in a new way. Instead of saying to myself, "I want to feel affluent," or "I want to feel divinely feminine," I went with affirmative phrasing: "I *am* affluent," and "I *am* divinely feminine." Ahhh. That felt better, warmer, closer.

Then I experimented with using nouns, rather than adjectives, and that felt even more vibrant and inspirational. So affluent became *affluence,* and divinely feminine became *The Divine Feminine.* Mmmm. Even closer to home.

These days, **I use affirmative and wishing phrases interchangeably.** Depending on my head and heart space, I might affirm that, "I am The Divine Feminine" or "I want to feel affluence." Either moves me forward.

As for "innovative" as a core desired feeling, I also put that to the test. For years "innovative" spurred me on. I'd sit at my desk about to start a new project, or stand backstage at a speaking gig, and I'd say to myself, "Innovative! Superpowers, activate!" To me, innovative meant being on my own creative edge—not necessarily being competitive in the marketplace. I didn't need to be different for the sake of being different; I just needed to keep my work fresh. It helped me push myself to do new things, to break my own rules. It helped me get stuff done.

But after years of feeling encouraged by "innovative" as a core desired feeling, it started to feel restrictive. I was becoming much more feminine-focused and relaxed in my approach to work, and "innovative" just felt too masculine and driven. "Creative"—which I had previously thought was too soft and too common—moved in and took over for innovative. Creative and I make a lot of awesome stuff together. This doesn't, for better or for worse, include baked goods.

"Connected" needed some refining as well. "In communion" felt less transactional and much more sacred and intimate.

CLAIMING MY DEEPEST DESIRE ONCE AND FOR ALL: JOY

So I came to this:

The Divine Feminine.
Affluence.
Creative.
In communion.

It felt like a gorgeous constellation of shining stars. But it still seemed like there was a spot to fill—a lead role, even. I was very aware that I wanted to feel light in my being, as up-to-date and current as possible, more fluidity, greater freedom, more . . . joy.

Joy. It's my deep belief that our true essence is pure joy. Every chance I get to interview a theologian or devout spiritual seeker, I ask, "So what do you think is the stuff of our true nature?" And when they reply, "Joy," I click my heels and say, "Ha! I *knew* it!" Joy.

Why hadn't that made it onto my list? Joy is my fundamental aspiration. Feeling light, feeling currents of energy, fluid, free. Each of these emotions stems from joy. It occurred to me that perhaps I'd been avoiding it all this time.

I used to think that cheery, consistently happy people were too "lite," too . . . in denial of something. Broody was more fascinating. Then I considered the fact that during the most excruciatingly difficult times in my life, forward motion came down to this declaration, this mantra: **I will do whatever it takes to feel joy.**

That resolve and devotion opened my life up so much wider than before. The learning brought me sweetness. I found new things—new theories, foods, cities, yoga poses, ideas, friends, new ways of seeing old friends—that ushered me into new dimensions of happiness. My greatest trials spurred me to make happiness a sacred priority.

And I figured out that joy is the clearest indicator of deep wellness. It's the result of our core vitality and our resilience.

Committing to joy as a core desired feeling would mean that I was declaring myself worthy of having everything that I wanted. It would tie me to a universal longing and to all of the other humans who share that longing. There would be no excuses for neglecting my Soul. Some dusty to-dos would have to be imploded to make way for more dynamic Soul imperatives. Some ambitions could die. Some things would have to give way to truer pursuits.

I would have to show up more freely.

I would have to desire more than ever.

Joy it is.

USING YOUR CORE DESIRED FEELINGS TO GUIDE WHAT YOU WANT TO DO, HAVE & EXPERIENCE

The fire has its flame and praises God.
The wind blows the flame and praises God.
In the voice we hear the word which praises God.
And the word, when heard, praises God.
So all of creation is a song of praise to God.

—Hildegard of Bingen

Desire presses ever forward unsubdued.

—Sigmund Freud

BRIDGING YOUR DESIRES TO YOUR INTENTIONS

Now we're going to make connections between how you want to feel and what will actually help you feel that way. This is the most critical part of the process. This is where we fully step up to our creative power and potential. I can't overstate this: when you're clear on how you want to feel and you set about generating those feelings, you take charge of your life and your happiness. This is the most consciously creative act of being human.

You're going to go through each of the life areas (wellness, relationships, and so on) and ask yourself what you want to have and experience in each area. But you're going to do it from a fresh mindset, in a new way—you're going to do it with your core desired feelings as the central goal.

Your desired feelings are dictating what you will set out to achieve.

We're working from the inside out, which is the opposite of how we've been trained to organize our lives. Typically we'd be aiming to "own a two-bedroom house in the city," with the unspoken (and often also unconscious) hope that we might feel something along the lines of "vitality" and "connected" when we got it. But that's backward. So we're going to ask ourselves what we need to do, experience, and have in order to feel the way we most want to feel.

It might be tempting in this part of the process to slip back into default goals—those things that we've been chasing somewhat mindlessly, out of social expectation or habit. By virtue of asking yourself what it will really take to feel the way you want, some of your long-held, external ambitions might fall away, or some of them may become clearer and dearer to you than ever before.

An example of desired feelings clarifying one's ambitions.

It might start like this: I want to feel vitality and to feel connected, deeply loving, and prosperous within the Relationships and Society of my life, so I want to own a two-bedroom house in the city.

But then you could realize that if you want vitality and to feel connected, deeply loving, and prosperous within the Relationships and Society of your life, maybe you *don't* actually need to own a two-bedroom house in the city. Just because it's a mainstream symbol of success, and your parents are expecting you to become a responsible homeowner, and common financial advice counsels that owning your residence is a sound investment doesn't mean it's right for you. When you get honest with yourself, maybe owning a home right now feels like a major burden to you. It doesn't make you feel a sense of vitality or prosperity at all. In fact, it makes you feel constricted and weighed down. What a revelation. So you scratch that goal off your list and replace it with something that is much more likely to help you feel connected, vitality, deeply loving, and prosperous in your Relationships and Society:

"One month with Sam in Costa Rica by the end of next year. Unplugged. Invite a bunch of friends to join us for the last week of the trip."

You keep renting. You start living.

Or, alternatively, your long-held dream might become clearer and dearer to you than ever before. Owning a two-bedroom house in the city is much more than just a material goal. You can see that it will allow you to feel more *connected* to yourself (a place to root and create) and connected to a community, which adds to your *vitality* in a big way. Creating a safe and beautiful home for your growing family is another way for you to express your *deep love,* and building your equity is definitely going to make you feel *prosperous.*

Indeed, this vision is right on track with your Soul. You decide to ramp up your savings plan for a down payment and meet with a Realtor next week for a chat about the neighborhood.

Your most desired feelings are the whole point.

I want you to keep this question in your heart for all time:

What do I need to do to feel the way I want to feel?

That's IT. That's the heart of this next exploration and the raison d'être of desire mapping.

In breath. Out breath. Here we go.

LIVELIHOOD & LIFESTYLE

career. money. work. home. style.
space. possessions. fashion. travel.
gifts. sustainability. resources.

If I want to feel this way [write your core desired feelings here]

within the realm of LIVELIHOOD & LIFESTYLE,
then I want to do, experience, and have the following:

BODY & WELLNESS

healing. fitness. food. rest & relaxation.
mental health. sensuality. movement.

If I want to feel this way [write your core desired feelings here]

within the realm of BODY & WELLNESS,
then I want to do, experience, and have the following:

CREATIVITY & LEARNING

artistic and self-expression.
interests. education. hobbies.

If I want to feel this way [write your core desired feelings here]

within the realm of CREATIVITY & LEARNING,
then I need to do, experience, and have the following:

RELATIONSHIPS & SOCIETY

romance. friendship. family.
collaboration. community. causes.

If I want to feel this way [write your core desired feelings here]

within the realm of RELATIONSHIPS & SOCIETY,
then I need to do, experience, and have the following:

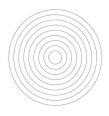

ESSENCE & SPIRITUALITY

soul. inner self. truth. intuition.
faith. practices.

If I want to feel this way [write your core desired feelings here]

within the realm of my ESSENCE & SPIRITUALITY,
then I need to do, experience, and have the following:

What do I need to do to feel the way I want to feel?

BRUTAL FACTS AND FEARS ABOUT GETTING WHAT YOU WANT

My core desired feelings

Go to the dark side for a minute. Get it out of your system.

What past failures are plaguing you?

What mistakes are you afraid to make again?

Which wounds are still healing?

What would the naysayers or your haughty inner critic say to stop you?

And what are the current tough circumstances, market conditions, or obstacles standing between you and what you want in every area of your life?

Let 'em tumble out however they come to you. Detox time.

POSITIVE AND INSPIRING THOUGHT FORMS THAT WILL ECLIPSE FEAR AND REV YOU UP

My core desired feelings

Now's the time to record helpful thought forms that can quell all the negative stuff you wrote out on the previous pages. Choose optimism. Think thoughts that feel good. Cheerlead yourself.

What are your favorite past successes?

Who are the people who adore and support you the most?

Who are the role models and mavericks who've proven that it can be done?

Riff out a list of high-energy, uplifting words. You can make bright, determined, feisty, resounding declarations.

BONUS! YOU GOT WHAT YOU WANT. ALREADY.

Clarity of desire, wants, feelings, havings, doings . . . you're getting the hang of it. Before we move into action mode, here's a beautiful notion to consider: You have a lot of what you want already—in places you may have over-looked, in different packaging than you expect, and hidden in plain sight.

And when you can appreciate the **indirect and subtle** ways in which Life is already delivering on your dreams, then you'll create more direct and obvious pleasures in your life, just the way you've been imagining them.

WHAT DO YOU WANT . . . THAT YOU ALREADY HAVE?

Review your desires. Look back at what you've said you want to feel, have, experience, and do. Pick a handful of those wants and write them down here.

Now, with each desire, think about where you already have that **quality, feeling, or experience** in your life—you might have to dig deep to find it. That's okay. You'll find it somewhere. Even if it's just a speck or a subtle sensation.

I want: *I want to laugh more with my man.* Currently, you're not laughing much with your man, which is why you're craving it, of course. But! Someone in your life *must* be filling your funny cup.

I already have: *Sally makes me laugh my ass off at least twice a week. Jack at work is good for a giggle every day. (Action note to self: Call Sally more. Thank her for making me laugh. Hang out with Jack at the water cooler.)* Focus on the laughter that you do have in your life.

Super duper appreciate what you've got that makes you feel good. **Resist the temptation to compare it to what you're lacking.** Just keep appreciating, appreciating, appreciating what's working, where it's working.

This practice is not only soothing, but it can also help you to fundamentally lighten the eff up.

I want: *I want an additional $500 every pay period.*

I already have: *I got money back from income taxes! I get a paid holiday next week. Now that I work at home on Fridays, I save 100 bucks a month on train fare and lunch out. (Affirmative note to self: My money/energy flow is increasing.)* You just found about 500 additional bucks in your life. More is sure to come, very possibly from sources you haven't even accounted for yet.

I want: *I want to spend more time in nature. I'm stuck in a cubicle, in a big city, and I'm going bonkers. Plus I can't get out of town right now.*

I already have: *Well, I'm bringing flowers in to work this week. Sleeping with the bedroom windows open. I'm sitting on my balcony to say prayers every night before bed. I'm framing those photos from my holiday in the Sierras. (Action note to self: Book that hiking trip in Maine NOW. No excuses.)*

Small things can be big acts of self-love that will boost you and help you make the bigger choices required to really go after your desires—like moving out of the city, apropos of the above example.

I want: *I want a good friend to tell my dreams to.*

I already have: *My journal, my dog, and my deaf grandma are all great listeners. I can tell them anything and everything about my dreams and they don't judge me. (Affirmative note to self: Even if I don't have a best friend who gets me, Life hears my dreams. Every single one.)*

Sometimes you really need to reach to find what's working in the realm of your desire. And the practice of identifying some positives might feel like you're collecting crumbs. Do it anyway. It will start to rinse away any lurking victim mentality or despair. Start somewhere.

Here's what happens when you find evidence of fulfillment and pleasure in your current reality (even if it's a stretch to do so):

› You take the neediness vibe out of your wants, and when you're less desperate, you will think more clearly and act more calmly.

› You ease up on the people around you.

› You generate gratitude—and gratitude is a transformative force.

> You might realize that you—and some of the people you love—are further along than you've been giving yourself—or them—credit for.

> Because you're appreciating more in your life, you'll cling less to what you want—and a loose grip helps everything breathe and come to life.

HELPFUL PEOPLE AND RESOURCES

How did the rose ever open its heart and give to this world all of its beauty?
It felt the encouragement of light against its being; otherwise we all remain too frightened.

—Hafiz

My core desired feelings

People who can help me live out my core desired feelings

People who are local, near to me, who I know directly and personally

Professionals, experts, service providers

Legendary thinkers and personalities (include their writing, programs, courses)

Deities, angels, spirits, spiritual forces

HOW WILL YOU GIVE OF YOURSELF?

To get what he wanted, a man had to give other people what they wanted.

—Dashiell Hammett, *Red Harvest*

My core desired feelings

You should be basking in the abundance of who you are by now. You have so much to give.

Where would you like to give your love and talent? Where can you pour out your talent and expertise in a way that will light you right up?

You don't have to commit to giving in all these ways or to all of the outlets you can give to. You can turn some of this into an intention or goal later in this process. For now, just free-flow about what's possible—it generally feels quite regenerative to look at where and how you can give.

DESIRE, MEET ACTION

Planning is essential. Plans are useless.

—Winston Churchill

If you want to be clear, act.

—Marcus Buckingham

This is where you sift through everything that you said you want to **do, experience, and have** in your life—and you choose **the most important of those intentions and goals** to go after.

We're going to keep this really simple.

ONLY CHOOSE THREE OR FOUR MAJOR INTENTIONS OR GOALS FOR THE YEAR

Here's my theory—feel free to burn it down or to make it your new religion: Significant intentions and goals take time to achieve, and a year flies by, so you have to FOCUS. It might ache a bit to put some intentions on the back burner. Naturally. But those wants can circle back for attention. And the momentum and satisfaction you'll gain from pulling off just a few amazing endeavors will far outweigh anything you could gain from doing a bunch of things halfway.

Set out to do three or four things this year with gusto and excellence, rather than doing a dozen things just sufficiently. Trust me on this.

CHOOSE LESS IF YOU NEED TO

And hey, if you're aiming to do something Herculean and stupendous this year, then by all means, make that your **singular focus.** This could be The Year of the Concert Tour; The Year We Built the House; The Year I Got a Promotion; The Year of Healing; The Year I Finished My Book.

TRUST YOUR HEART

And as I suggested when we started this journey, you can let the goal selecting be easier if you allow yourself to **trust your inner guidance and don't worry so much about getting it "right."** Yes, there could be some deliberation over choosing the best goals, and you might let out a heavy sigh when you decide to put one of your wishes on hold in favor of being able to focus on another. (Focus. It hurts so good.) But don't back down from the process at this stage. This is the crest of your creativity. Ride it.

CHOOSING

The most powerful question to ask yourself when you consider which intentions or goals to focus on:

WHAT AM I MOST EXCITED ABOUT?

That's the key. This is about what lights you up the most. It's about what thrills you the most. Never mind that it may also be daunting and unreasonable. Out of your various intentions or goals, what are you the most enthusiastic about? Enthusiasm is a special emotion. It tends to stir up and carbonate all other positive feelings.

Other questions to vet your intentions by.

Your selections should not hinge solely on the following questions, but these questions will help you get clearer on what excites you the most.

> How will this affect other people?

> How can I work with people I like to get this done?

> Does this help me generate more than one of my core desired feelings?

> How would I feel if I died without doing this?

> What will take the least amount of effort to pull off?

> What has the highest earning potential?

> What will require the largest amount of money?

› How could this affect the next five to ten years of my life?

› What is the scariest thing to do?

› Do I feel I was born to do this?

IN CASE YOU'RE SCARED TO MAKE SOME CHOICES

Everything is progress. I've said it before, I'll say it again, and again: the universe is always expanding—that includes you. Errors, missteps, detours—it's all progress.

> I chose and my world was shaken. So what? The choice may have been mistaken; the choosing was not.
>
> —Stephen Sondheim

You can change your mind, anytime. Just like that.

Just do something. Motion is better than stasis. When you take action, you learn, you build skills, you get freer. When you stay still because you're afraid to make a move, your self-worth wanes, your doubts fester and breed more doubts, your courage atrophies. It's not pretty. Suit up and head out.

CHOOSE THREE OR FOUR MAJOR INTENTIONS AND GOALS FOR THE YEAR

My core desired feelings

You're putting your core desired feelings at the center of your life. Yes, yes, you are. You know how you want to feel. And you've got a really good idea of what you can do, have, and experience—and think and believe—to help yourself feel that way.

Now you're going to take aim and devote yourself to actualizing what you want the most.

Go through each of the life areas (LIVELIHOOD, SPIRITUALITY, and so on) and REVIEW what you said you want to do, experience, and have in that area in order to feel your core desired feelings.

Out of all these things, which are the most exciting to you? Which of them makes you feel the way you want to feel? Now home in on three or four of the most potent feel-good opportunities that you would like to actualize this year.

MY INTENTIONS AND GOALS FOR THIS YEAR

ACTION SHEETS

Yearly achievements happen through daily choices and monthly aims.

I suggest you do a MONTHLY CHECK-IN and a WEEKLY action list. I've created formatted sheets you can write on directly within this workbook or refer to while writing your answers on a separate sheet of paper. (You can also print these out from *The Desire Map* website in a variety of sizes.)

Decide what you need to do each month to move closer to your three or four intentions or goals for the year. I prefer to do this just one month at a time, rather than filling in objectives for twelve months at once.

For many of us, core desired feelings are an entirely new way of steering our lives and setting goals. **You'll have to keep reminding yourself:** your primary intention is to feel good, and all of your external objectives exist in order to help you feel your core desired feelings.

So when you sit down for this monthly check-in, you're going to look at your desired feelings as the driver.

Keep this important question in mind every week and month when you ink out your to-dos:

How can I reach my long-term vision in ways that feel . . . ? [Insert your desired feelings.] What you're feeling along your journey is what creates the result.

This question will help you adjust your actions and behaviors in order to get to your goal. You evaluate, affirm, or adjust your to-dos and your intentions according to what you think will generate your desired feelings.

Using your desired feelings as a guidance system isn't about being loosey-goosey with your intentions so that you give up when the going gets rough. It's about finding a way to feel good every step of the way. It's about accomplishing things in life-affirming, rather than Soul-sucking, ways.

MONTHLY CHECK-IN

MONTH:

My core desired feelings

My intentions and goals for this year

My intentions and goals for this month

THIS WEEK

What I'll do to generate my core desired feelings
and help myself reach this month's intentions and goals

My core desired feelings

LIVELIHOOD & LIFESTYLE

BODY & WELLNESS

CREATIVITY & LEARNING

RELATIONSHIPS & SOCIETY

ESSENCE & SPIRITUALITY

A few positive declarations

Helpful people to connect with

People to be of service to

DESIRE AS A PRACTICE

I'm sending you off now. To pioneer. To burn brightly. To serve. To love . . . your life, and the world. This is my last lecture of the season. I'm going to tell you everything I know about making this stick. I pray that it's useful.

AS A MATTER OF COURSE

1. Plan your week or month by your core desired feelings. "What do I need to do this week to generate my core desired feelings?" Or, "What can I do this month to feel . . . " I like to keep this really simple. I write out three to five actions each week that are on track with both my desired feelings and my goals (goals which are sourced from my desired feelings to begin with).

I like to scope out the coming week on Fridays, because weekends are good for my mental health, and planning for the week on a Monday is the surest way to get behind the eight ball. (Never, ever plan your week out on a Monday.)

2. Recite your core desired feelings to yourself before you fall asleep and before you get out of bed in the morning. This is so quick and simple to do, and these are the perfect times for your subconscious to be attended to. If you're on a roll, go beyond your core desired feelings and just keep riffing on any and all positive feelings that come to mind. Each one is a wish and a confirmation of your true nature.

3. Put it in writing. Sometimes I write my desired feelings on my bathroom mirror using those erasable whiteboard markers. I also have them on a sticky note on my computer monitor, and I write them out once a week in my day planner, or I use the action sheets.

People tell me that they have their desired feelings posted in view in their offices, on their fridges, and on the dashboards of their cars.

4. Use your core desired feelings as a **mantra** during meditation and/or throughout the day as a calming, centering, inspiring reminder to yourself. Repeat them twelve times with your eyes closed (or three, or a hundred). Or, do a quickie desire booster, and before you get out of the car, or make a phone call, or walk through the door—before you transition into the next thing you're about to do—speak your desired feelings to yourself.

5. Sleep with this book by your bed. Keep it close to you, not on a bookshelf out of reach. And not because I want to hang out in your bedroom with you, but because seeing it in the morning and at night will remind you that you're a desire ninja.

6. On the last day of every month, or twice yearly, or when you change your clock for daylight savings time (you get the picture—some regular interval(s) in the course of your year), pull out *The Desire Map* book and **reread what you wrote.**

7. Tell someone how you most want to feel.

8. Ask for angelic or multidimensional advice and write out the reply you receive. This doesn't have to be as woo-woo as it sounds. Or it could be. Sometimes I sit down with my notebook and ask the universe, "So what do you want to tell me?" And I just let the pen roll. I don't care if I'm making it up, or if I'm actually channeling Cleopatra. It's another way to access my Soul's knowing and it's always comforting and revelatory.

9. Listen to positive stuff. One of my favorite ways to learn and to soothe my Soul is to listen to audiobooks while I'm in the kitchen or the bathtub.

I like knowing that if I get distracted or start talking with whoever's around, my subconscious is still absorbing that good stuff. I also like that even though he's too young to understand it all, my kid is immersed in good thinking. And the same goes for my man. He's not too young to understand, of course, but he'd rather be listening to the news, and this is my way of sneaking some Soul vitamins into his day, too.

My favorite audio programs are anything by metaphysical teachers Abraham-Hicks, meditation instructor Reggie Ray, Buddhist teacher Pema Chödrön, poet/theologian John O'Donahue, and author of *Women Who Run With the Wolves,* Clarissa Pinkola Estés.

As you know, *The Desire Map*—and all the contemplations herein—are available on audio. It's hours of power, people.

In addition, *The Fire Starter Sessions* audio program is seven-plus hours of motivation and love, which you can download from audible.com.

WHEN THINGS SUCK

1. When you're feeling far from your Soul zone and something shitty is happening . . . **fully accept it.** I know, I know. Believe me, I *know.* This could sound naïvely flaky and downright fucking impossible. It usually is. And yet! This counsel is at the heart of most Eastern mysticism. Don't deny what's real—face it. Don't resist the moment—merge into it so that you can fully experience the truth of what's happening.

And divinely enough, if you can be with the pain or negativity rather than pushing it away, it tends to dissolve faster so that you can move on.

Presence is *the* vantage point in life.

2. When you're not feeling the way you want, you can say this: **"I'm really looking forward to feeling . . . "** Even if you're totally steamed or really discouraged, just uttering positive, future-focused words can create a shift.

First, of course, you need to look your negative feelings in the face—out of respect. It's not productive to go straight from the sucky circumstance and *mindlessly* into the positive thoughts. Feel how much it sucks and *then* choose a brighter thought form.

3. You can also use this phrase in almost any bind: **"I'm clear that I want to feel . . . "** It's incredibly grounding, and it also works well when conveying to other people what you want from a situation—especially in an intimate relationship. Stating how you want to feel helps you steer clear of criticism and complaining about yourself or other people.

4. When things don't go the way you want them to, you can say to yourself, **"Well, at least I'm even clearer about how I want to feel now."** Or perhaps all you can eke out is, **"Maybe I'll be grateful for this someday."** That's a step in the right direction.

5. Refer to your positive thought forms page in this book. Memorize them like the invocations that they are. Or! Have someone else read them out loud to you. It's a bit strange to hear your own rah-rah read back to you, but it's good brain food, I promise.

HELP EACH OTHER

I felt it shelter to speak to you.

—Emily Dickinson

1. Meet up. After the release of *The Fire Starter Sessions,* book clubs and groups started springing up from Fargo to London, in living rooms, cafés, via Facebook and Skype. *The Desire Map* is also an experience that could be enriched by group support—whether it's you and your girlfriend in person, or a group from across the country meeting on the phone once a week.

Check out *The Desire Map* site for some guidelines and real-life examples of how people are running face-to-face and virtual groups.

2. Cheer each other on. You know yourself best (and you know yourself even better after desire mapping), so do whatever works for you to create accountability around these actions and plans. If you're good at following through on your own, wonderful. If you need an accountability partner/buddy, then make that happen first.

WANT TO START A DESIRE MAP GROUP? INTRODUCING THE WORLD'S BIGGEST BOOK CLUB EVER

For one-on-one connecting and or groups of greatness: book clubs, meet-ups, bloggers, soul seekers and conversationalists—whether virtual or in person . . .

The Desire Map is more than a program for goals with Soul—it's a life philosophy. So your Desire Map gathering will be more than just a "book club." But you knew that already. It will be what you want it to be. Highly structured or loose. Section by section or one life area per meeting. A weekend in a cabin with girlfriends or a year of discovery.

Your Desire Map group is support system meets book club. A not-so-secret society of Desire Mappers in your real-life hood or your favorite virtual platform. A gathering of seekers, entrepreneurs, nine-to-fivers, mamas and their men, yogis, hard workers, light lovers, of people with a distinctly uncommon purpose—**to feel the way they truly want to feel in every area of their life.**

A weekly potluck, a monthly meetup, a seasonal solstice soiree, the event of a lifetime, or just a Thursday night ritual. Whatever, whenever, whyever you want it to be. Give it some thrust, but don't overthink it. Make a date.

IDEAS ON HOW TO STRUCTURE YOUR DESIRE MAPPING GROUP (REMEMBER: IT ONLY TAKES TWO PEOPLE TO MAKE A GROUP)

Start the meeting while people are gathering with some desire-inspired music. You can head to DanielleLaPorte.com to access a number of playlists.

There are a number of companion audio programs to *The Desire Map* from me and Sounds True—both to purchase and for free. You could open up a meeting with an audio kickoff from me on the chapter or a guided reflection of your choice.

Go Zen. Your Desire Map Group could meet to simply READ, WATCH or LISTEN in appreciative silence.

Pass the mic. Everyone in your group could be responsible for leading a meeting—at least once. Assign each member a section, at random—or let 'em choose a topic they want to dig into.

Invite special guests. A fabulous life coach. A psychologist. An eccentric artist.

LET THE CONTENT DO THE WORK

At each meeting, you could concentrate on one or two of the worksheets, like Sensations of Positivity, Gratitude & Dissatisfaction, Core Desired Feelings, Brutal Facts & Fears.

As you know, *The Desire Map* is two books in one. Book One is the philosophy, Book Two is your workbook. Pick a chapter from the theory section to discuss. Plan some key questions and talking points beforehand. For example . . .

DISCUSSION POINTS FOR INTENTIONS AND GOALS

› Danielle prefers the word "intention" over "goal." How does each of these words make you feel? Why do you think that is?

› "I only want to hit my targets if the aiming and the hitting both feel good." Is there something you've been pushing for and the pushing does not feel good?

› Talk about the pressure to "have it all."

› The section about letting go of goals is liberating but scary. Who is making the decision to let some goals go?

CONCEPTS AND QUESTIONS FOR STIRRING CONVERSATION

Do a free-for-all response round for each of these concepts and questions. What thoughts or feelings do they stir up? People can have two minutes to respond, just to get the energy warmed up—or you can keep the floor open and see where the conversation takes you.

> Can you accomplish great things in life without having set goals?

> A feeling is much stronger than a thought.

> Worry is useless.

> Don't judge how you want to feel.

> Why do we push away good feelings?

> You are not your feelings.

> What's your version of "having it all"?

> What motivates you? What inspires you?

> A strong mind looks forward—not backwards.

> Joy is your true nature.

THE MOST IMPORTANT QUESTION YOU CAN ASK EACH OTHER IN BETWEEN MEETINGS
What are you doing TODAY to feel the way you want to feel?

Text each other. Call and leave a message. Keep asking and reminding each other that fulfilled desires grow from this profoundly simple question.

"I'm doing a wardrobe clearout (*Sex and the City* style, with girlfriends and champagne). I'm getting rid of anything that doesn't help me feel **Radiant and Joyful** (everything that is worn-out, ill-fitting, or belonging in my former corporate life)." —Belinda

"I made a beautiful meal for my sister this morning: **Connection.** I'm wearing my favorite scarf: **Radiant.**" —Stacey

"I'm organizing my office: **Empowered.**" —Jackie

"I'm taking a meditation class: **Inspired.** Definitely seeing family and having friend dates: **Joyful.**" —Ellie

"I'm starting hiphop dance classes this week and **Badass** is flowing through my veins." —Cynthia

"I adopted three kittens. I feel **ALIVE!**" —Paula

STORY OF A DESIRE MAPPING GROUP

"Our group meets face to face, once a month, in Calgary. We've also connected with people in Portland and Toronto, and we might start to include them virtually (via Skype) at our meetings. If not, we plan to share our progress with them through email so we maintain a connection.

Before *The Desire Map,* our emphasis was on 'What do you wanna get done?' This was fine and we were definitely making moves and accomplishing big things, but it was a one-dimensional approach. Kinda flat. So now the key question is, **'How do you want to feel and what decisions are you going make to support those feelings?'**

These meetings are one of the only places we can come together and not be a mom or a wife or a job. We can just be. Women. Sharing, connecting, and simply being with each other. We talk about things that matter, making changes in our lives and getting the things we want, feeling good at every step along the way.

Last night someone said, 'I wanna lose weight.' Her body language was *bleh* when she said it. But when one of us asked her how she wanted to feel when she lost the weight, her body language shifted immediately and she excitedly said, 'I want to feel pretty.'

Seeing that was a great lesson for all of us. Our emphasis now is on the feeling, not the doing. The doing part happens, but it's not the driver anymore. Our feelings are the engine—and that feels so good!" —Lana Wright, Calgary

GOT A BLOG? LIGHT IT UP

Jamie Ridler sums book blogging up like this:

"The concept behind a book blogging is that a group of bloggers work their way through a book, sharing their experiences by posting on their own blog and by reading what other participants are sharing. You can choose to share as much, or as little, as you like. The process is free, self-directed, and shared in community."

In other words, use *The Desire Map* as your art-making and value-giving inspiration. It's fodder for your blog content, fuel for your shareable teachings. Blog regularly as part of your group (or individual) process.

MEETING VIRTUALLY

There are Skype group video calls, Google Hangout, or free conference telephone lines. You can find or create Desire Map groups on DanielleLaPorte.com.

MEETING IN PERSON

Meet somewhere inspiring. With plenty of parking. Depart at dawn for a two-hour hike. Consider somewhere accessible, central, with built-in childcare. Dining hall at IKEA, anyone? If you've got writerly, word-smitten people in your posse, go somewhere with tables and Wi-Fi.

Or keep it simple. Meet at home: yours, theirs, or a new pad every time. Revive the art of the potluck—or the slumber party. Consider: Wheelchair accessibility. Temperature. Bathrooms. Noise level. Lighting. Snacks + drinkables. Neighborhood vibe. Maximum comfort and joy.

WHEN? WHENEVER

Tonight. Tomorrow. On your lunch break. After yoga class. The third Sunday of every month, right after your interfaith seminary brunch. On Whiskey Wednesday at your local dive.

If your group members are ultra-busy-CEO-of-ME-types, offer them three date and time options before your first meeting. Get a consensus. Firm it up. And email out reminders a few days before each meeting.

Hey love,

A reminder: our next Desire Mapping group meet-up is on DATE at TIME at PLACE.

We'll meet for one hour. I'll have vegan truffles. BYOKombucha.

We're going to be diving into NAME OF SECTION / PAGE NUMBERS.

Read it already? Superb. Not yet? No worries.

I know—we're busy. We're fried. I, for one, could seriously use a roots touchup.

But this group is about our LIVES—our desires, our dreams, our most urgent ambitions. Our group matters. YOU matter.

Be there.

YOUR NAME

HOW TO RALLY A GROUP

Start with the usual suspects. Your friends, family, and inner orbit of trust. Prag-o-matic: make a list of twenty people who adore you. Tap each one with a lovingly crafted invitation. Shower them with praise. Be encouraging.

> "Hey, sister, remember that Goals with Soul video by Danielle LaPorte that I sent you? I'm starting a reading-group-quest-for-enlightenment kinda thing. And you're my first member."

> "Hey, honey, you know how you're always complaining that you don't get outta the house enough? I'm starting a book club. And I found you a sitter for the night of our first meeting. Polish your boots. No backing out."

> "Dude. You're the most fiery, always-in-a-good-mood human I know. I'm leading a life + career + joy circle, and I need you to be there to show us how it's done. Say YES."

Facebook

Announce your intention to start a group to your friends and fans on Facebook. Connect with others in the Desire Map group on Facebook. Once you find your people, you can branch off and either meet online or in person. You might want to start your own private Facebook group and invite your friends to join it. Fan the flames with daily invitations on your wall.

Twitter

Head to Twitter to tweet your desire for some round-table revelry, and use the #DesireMap hashtag to see and be seen by other Desire Mappers. Your people will find you.

Meetup

Create a desire-inspired event on MeetUp.com. There are eight million-plus users on this social nexus, with forums, membership sites, and e-course communities.

Find Desire Map Groups to Join

Desire Map groups are springing up all over the world. Head to DanielleLaPorte.com/bookclub to create or find a group that works for you.

If you can contribute anything about how you're running your group, please email support@daniellelaporte.com and let us know. We want your stories! Your pictures! Your questions! Your ideas!

ONE MORE THING

This would be the perfect place for a self-help writer to tell you to GO FOR IT! Or maybe suggest a reward/subliminal torture system for staying on track. *Buy a new pair of shoes when you feel your core desired feelings for three days in a row! If you don't make it to the gym every day this week, you have to pay your brother a hundred bucks—that'll get your ass in gear. Win at the game of life!*

But I'm not that guy. I'm ambitious, but I'm a softie. And I'm practical. Some of us really want to be truly alive. And some of us are more intent on just getting through life so we can die. You've got to move toward it—Life, that is. Truth, light, love. And no system, not even *The Desire Map* is going to guarantee that you'll choose Life.

You are the guarantor of your bliss.

I want this to work for you—and by work I mean, I want you to be joyful, to know your true luminous nature, to leave things better than you found them. I want you to fall madly in love with being alive. And I'll admit that I'd also love for you to be really productive on the planet. But that's just my trip.

Be what you want. All that you are.

Be what feels good.

you are more than your name
your frame
your DNA
more plenty than all that you have
given birth
to
big big wishes!
you are even bigger
imagine that
(imagine anything)
and you are more
you are gone gone gone beyond
the beyond of what
started This All
I pray you
desire temples of peace
and benevolent tsunamis of love
and that you realize your size in relation to this universal
declaration:
I desire . . .
you are the that
and the and
the core
and the more
ever expanding
desire . . .

THANK YOU

There was a woman who kindly accosted me when I got offstage from a speaking gig. "That desire stuff you talked about is fucking awesome!" To that woman, whoever you are, *Thank you.* You gave me an idea.

Harper. You're the best thing I ever decided to make.

Angie Wheeler is the guardian angel of my business. I can't overstate how capable she is as a true production partner, and how lovely of a human being she is. In the most practical sense, Angie makes my dreams come true. Her smarts and heart are woven into every inch of this.

During the entire process of creating this program, I had almost weekly Soul sessions with **Hiro Boga** to help me access both my truth and my stamina. Her devotion and skill as an energy alchemist have been among the greatest gifts of this journey.

Ann Moller is this program's original editor. When she gave me edits on the first draft, I teared up with relief. *I've found her!* I thought. Ann did for this what great editors do for any book: she made it immensely better.

Alex Miles Younger raised the bar for great book design.

With tremendous integrity, vision, and agility, my new family at Sounds True—with an extra-deep bow to **Nancy Smith, Tami Simon, and Haven Iverson**—has been an absolute blessing.

If I didn't talk with **Candis Hoey** every week I'd be a crazy lady. She keeps me real. **Navjit Kandola** sends me light, which goes straight to my heart. **Lianne Raymond** let me know that "all my other stuff was good, but this is what she was really waiting for." **Gabrielle Bernstein, Terri Cole, Michael Ellsberg, Chela Davison, Eric Handler, Jonathan Fields, Alexandra Franzen, Tanya Geisler, Chris Guillebeau, Scott Johnson, Kate Northrup, Nisha Moodley, Linda Sivertsen, Donna and Brad VanEvery,** and **Danielle Vieth** are all cheerleaders of the highest order.

Kris Carr and **Marie Forleo** make me think that I must have done something good in a past life to be honored this time 'round with their powerful love and support.

This program has been a journey with a number of destinations, and each stop and turn along the way brought new insight and professional perspectives—and encouragement—notably from **Brettne Bloom**, **Mary Choteborsky,** and **Tina Constable** at Random House/Crown, **Lisa DiMona**, and **Don Franzen**.

There was a support crew that helped me cross the finish line: **Reema Al-Zaben, Erin Blaskie**, **Jenn Rose Orajay**, **Annika Martins**, and **Hannah Brencher**.

Dozens of people over the years have endured my willy-nilly worksheets and abstract questions. I hope I've made all of you early adopters proud.

And YOU. Perhaps you're one of the hundreds of people who answered my questions on Facebook or Twitter. You told me what you thought of goal-setting. You publicly shared your most wanted feelings (incredible). You sent me "this really works!" messages, and you got your partners, friends, and co-workers desire mapping. You blew me away. You helped make this what it is.

And now you're here. *Thank you so very very much for coming.*